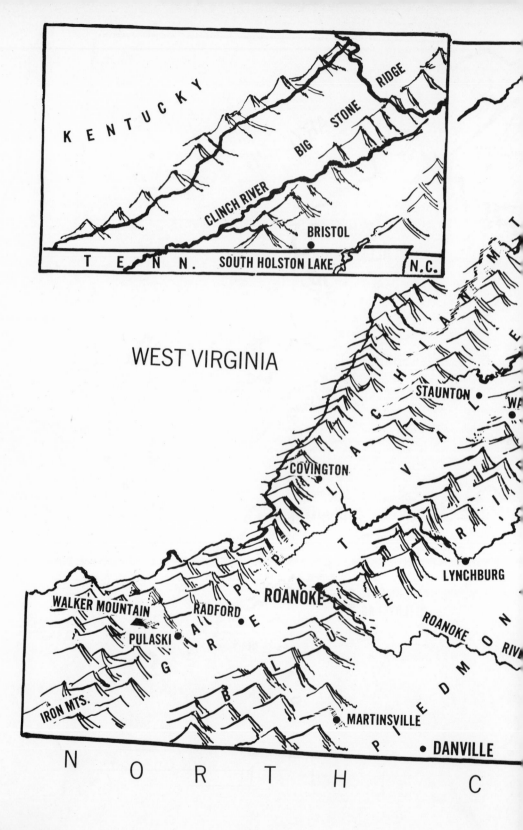

KENTUCKY

RIDGE

BIG STONE

CLINCH RIVER

BRISTOL

T E N N.   SOUTH HOLSTON LAKE

N.C.

WEST VIRGINIA

STAUNTON

COVINGTON

LYNCHBURG

ROANOKE

WALKER MOUNTAIN

RADFORD

PULASKI

ROANOKE RIVER

IRON MTS.

MARTINSVILLE

DANVILLE

N O R T H   C

VIRGINIA

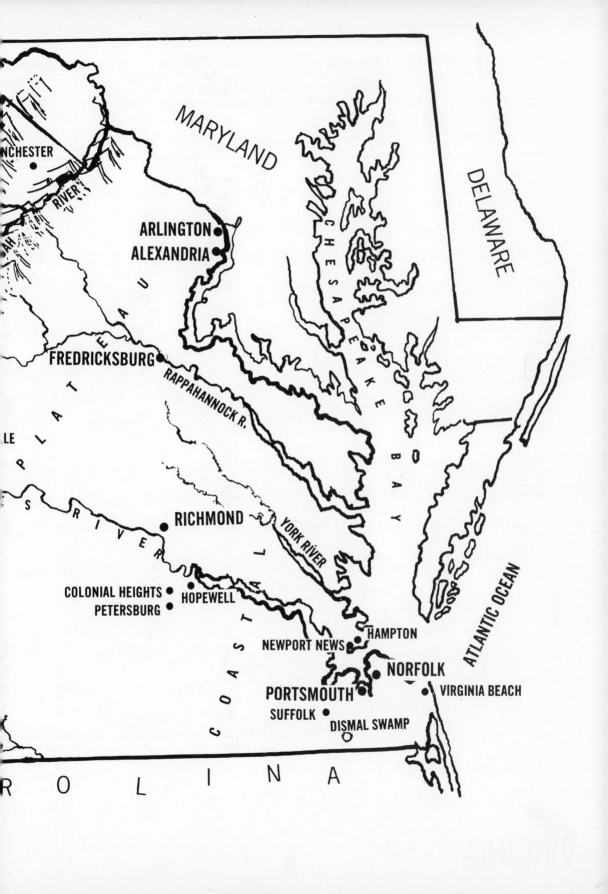

10th
State to join the Union

MT. VERNON
FLOWERING DOGWOOD
STATE FLAG
JAMES MONROE

VIRGINIA
by Michael Frome

Virginia—site of the first, permanent English-speaking colony in the New World, home of eight United States Presidents, battleground of historic Revolutionary and Civil War encounters, cradle of many of the liberties on which our nation is built.

Michael Frome explores Virginia today through her history, geography, industry, natural resources and people. As we travel through the state, we come on landmarks that are constant reminders of the part Virginia played in the shaping of the United States. Skillfully, Mr. Frome examines these landmarks and their significance—events, places, meetings—and explains how they contributed toward making Virginia the state it is today.

Through the book, whether discussing Virginia's early days or the present, Michael Frome keeps us aware of the beauty and variety of Virginia's land from ocean to mountain.

VIR

CONSULTANT: Marian Nesbitt
Elementary Supervisor, Richmond Public Schools

STATES OF THE NATION

GINIA

by Michael Frome

COWARD-McCANN, INC.   NEW YORK

To William and Michele,
my two young Virginians,
and to
Sam P. Weems,
their adopted uncle,
who has devoted a lifetime to making the
Blue Ridge Parkway
a place of delight and learning for all people.

PHOTO CREDITS

Colonial Williamsburg, pages 34 (painting by Sidney King), 38, 42-43
Daily News, Middleboro, Kentucky, page 103
Dementi Studio, pages 40, 59, 75, 81
Fort Monroe Casemate Museum, pages 52-53
Information Center, Fredericksburg, pages 90-91
Jamestown Foundation, pages 30, 33 (Thomas L. Williams)
Royster Lyle, Lexington, page 107
Mariners' Museum, pages 13, 23 (John L. Lochhead)
National Park Service, Blue Ridge Parkway, page 114
Newport News Shipbuilding Photo, page 14
Norfolk and Western Railway Co., title page, 101
Photo Craftsman, pages 10-11, 20
Portsmouth Chamber of Commerce, page 65
U. S. Dept. of the Interior, National Park Service, pages 49, 72
U. S. Forest Service, pages 84, 106, 109, 111
U. S. Navy, page 15
Virginia Chamber of Commerce, (Flournoy) 18, 24, 58, 61, 67; (Jim Corbett) 27, 41
Virginia Dept. of Conservation and Economic Development, pages 7, 9, 46, 55, 70-71, 95, 104-105

Jacket
Mt. Vernon, *Dr. Ralph H. Anderson, from Shostal*
Dogwood, *Virginia Dept. of Conservation and Economic Development*
Virginia State Flag, *Reprinted with permission of the copyright owner, F. E. Compton, division of Encyclopaedia Britannica, Inc., Chicago, Illinois*
James Monroe, *Virginia Dept. of Conservation and Economic Development*

Maps, Robert Gray

Library of Congress Catalog Card Number: AC 65-20392
PRINTED IN THE UNITED STATES OF AMERICA
082012

CONTENTS

Chapter I

Gateway from the Sea

A breeze blows, a salt sea breeze.

Overhead, a jet plane from the mighty Norfolk Naval Base soars to a distant rendezvous.

The waters are filled with all kinds of vessels — an aircraft carrier, a gigantic cargo liner, a freighter carrying newsprint from Finland, a coal barge, a fishing trawler plowing into the open sea with chattering gulls diving around it.

This is the gateway to Virginia, approaching from the Atlantic Ocean. It is one of the busiest water roadways of the world. You can see plenty of automobiles, too, driving north and south across the broad Chesapeake Bay. At least, you can see them part of the time, when they are on the gleaming causeways, or low bridges, above the surface of the water. But then they disappear into connecting tunnels beneath the ship channels. The cars move swiftly, covering the seventeen and a half miles across the water in less than a half hour. Truly a marvel of the mechanical age and a great engineering feat.

Chesapeake Bay Bridge-Tunnel

Looking at this teeming activity, it seems impossible that shipping in these coastal waters once was harassed by pirates. But for years there was no peace until the notorious Blackbeard was caught and killed in 1718. It was an exciting encounter. Lieutenant Robert Maynard, learning that Blackbeard and his men were hiding in an inlet on the coast of North Carolina, set after him from these waters with a crew of sailors in two small ships.

When Maynard caught up with Blackbeard, they fought a fierce battle, hand to hand. Finally the lieutenant killed him, cut off the pirate's head, and fastened it to the bowsprit of his ship. When he reached the port of Bath in North Carolina there was great rejoicing at the sight, for Blackbeard had inflicted fear and terror on villages all along the coast. From there the pirate crew was taken to Williamsburg, the capital of colonial Virginia, where they were tried and hanged.

That was long ago. But even before 1718, something more dramatic and important happened here.

Two sharp capes of land jut between the Atlantic Ocean and the Chesapeake Bay, like the two sides of an open gate. On the sandy dune of the southern cape, the first permanent English settlers in America waded ashore April 26, 1607. They erected a wooden cross of thanksgiving after four uncertain months afloat.

They named the southern area Cape Henry, in honor of the Prince of Wales, and the northern point of land Cape Charles, for the second son of King James. For the King himself they would name their settlement, a few miles farther inland, "James Towne."

It was the greatest event in the history of Virginia, and one of the major events in the history of the world. It was the beginning of the English-speaking colony that would become a free nation, the United States of America. This settlement was to become the cradle of many of the liberties on which our nation is built.

The gateway to Virginia from the sea and the place where its history began is in the section known as the Coastal Plain, or Tidewater — named because the ocean tides flow and ebb in the wide rivers all across this eastern one-fourth of the state.

Nature is the strongest influence in the Tidewater, as in all Virginia. It shapes most boundaries of our state: the ocean at the east, the great mountain barriers of Appalachia at the west, and the Potomac River on the north and northeast. But Nature does much more than chart geography. It determines where men shall live, the foods they shall eat, how they shall travel and earn their livings, the kinds of houses they build and the kind of recreation they seek. This was true in the beginning of settlement in the Tidewater; and it is true today in ways that make this a fascinating region of America, filled with history, and adventure on the land and sea.

Lighthouse at Cape Henry

From the ocean gateway, the broad waters of Chesapeake Bay extend 195 miles to the north. Not only did the first English to settle Virginia sail between the two capes, but so did the first Marylanders, when they came in 1634 to establish a haven for religious freedom.

The Bay is a great inland sea, covering nearly four times the area of Rhode Island. Its jagged shoreline, carved and cleft, is over 5,000 miles long. It is dotted with islands, some inhabited, but others are refuges of ducks and geese and other wild marsh birds. The Bay divides the Tidewater into two parts. On the ocean side is the Eastern Shore, shared by two counties of Virginia at the slender lower tip and on the north by portions of Maryland and Delaware. On the inland side, rivers and streams feeding into the Bay split the Tidewater land again into peninsulas, or "necks."

Around the Bay country, in a land flat as Holland, are many strange

Coastal plain of the Tidewater

and varied sights, of a sort not often seen elsewhere. The land is shared by clam diggers, oystermen, fishermen, yachtsmen, poultrymen, cabbage and tomato farmers, by wealthy people who have restored two-hundred-year-old houses, and by duck hunters and ducks — canvasbacks, mallards, pintails and black ducks by the thousands.

Scattered about the Bay and its tributaries are lighthouses built to guide mariners through fog and storm. From a distance some Chesapeake Bay lighthouses look like oversized bottles bobbing in the water. Others resemble fat little doll houses on stilts.

Some Virginia lighthouses have been famous in history, like the Old Lighthouse at Cape Henry, the first one erected by the government of the United States, back in 1792. But all have played their parts — and those that remain still do — in shaping the culture of a state that lives by the sea.

Chapter 2

The Mariners' Virginia

A gigantic old lighthouse lens, bigger than a lifeboat, is on display at the world-famous Mariners' Museum on the banks of the James River at Newport News, a few miles inland from the ocean. The lens comes from the Hog Island Lighthouse on the Eastern Shore of Virginia. It is part of the museum treasurehouse, devoted to the culture of the sea.

This museum could hardly have a more fitting location than the tip of the peninsula formed between the James and the York Rivers facing Chesapeake Bay.

The town of Hampton, north around the tip, is the center of Virginia's fishing fleet. Hundreds of boats bring in blue crabs, oysters and loads of fish. The Hampton trawlers are venturesome, working their way out into the ocean and as far north as the New England fishing grounds. But adventure is in the Hampton tradition. Settled in 1610, just three years after Jamestown, it is the oldest English-speaking settlement in the New World still in existence. It is the home of the

Inside the Mariners' Museum

Shipyard at Newport News

Hampton Institute, which trained Booker T. Washington and many others who blazed new trails for the Negro people.

The wonderful Mariners' Museum was established in 1930 by a man who loved the sea, and especially Chesapeake Bay and the waters of Virginia. His name was Archer M. Huntington, and he was owner of the Newport News Shipbuilding and Drydock Company. This firm manufactured the SS *United States,* the largest passenger liner ever built in our country, and the USS *Enterprise,* the only nuclear-powered aircraft carrier.

Mr. Huntington was interested in more than money. He appreciated nature, art and history. He wrote poetry about the wonders of being alive. He fell in love with a famous sculptress, Anna Hyatt, and married her. Mr. Huntington looked out the office window of his great shipyard and walked along the banks of the James and felt the romance of these waters and the romance of the waters they merge with all over the world.

From his window he saw the hundreds of bustling wharves and docks laden with tobacco, grain and ores. He could see the railway terminal

14

U.S. Atlantic Fleet at Norfolk

that connects the coal fields in the mountains with specially designed coal piers. He looked across the busy waters known as Hampton Roads to Norfolk and Portsmouth, the twin cities separated by the Elizabeth River. It was once said the ships were so thick you could cross from Norfolk to Portsmouth, from deck to deck, without getting your feet wet. Warships of all sizes were at their moorings in the Norfolk Naval Shipyard, headquarters of the Atlantic Fleet and the largest naval base in the world.

But Mr. Huntington, being a visionary as well as a businessman, saw more than the large scene before his eyes, and more than the present. He went down to watch an oyster tonger near the wide mouth of the James River, largest, most prolific oyster bed in Chesapeake Bay. In this particular section the oysters are small, and are harvested to be transplanted in other Virginia waters, where they grow large and fat. Harvesting is hard, for the two long tongs must be moved back and forth with short strokes to scrape the oysters from their beds deep in the water. The tonger is a waterman, too, thought Mr. Huntington; his little craft is part of the culture of the sea.

15

Mr. Huntington thought of the past, of the maritime history of the James River and Chesapeake Bay. It began with the Indians in their canoes, followed by the three small English ships heading upstream to Jamestown in 1607, and Captain John Smith, the footloose adventurer, who explored and mapped the Bay.

Mr. Huntington thought of the French fleet sailing into the Bay and up the river to Yorktown to help win the battle that ended the Revolutionary War. He imagined the British sloops that advanced up the Bay to camp on Tangier Island before the attack on Washington in the War of 1812. He thought of the Civil War and the battle between the *Virginia* and the *Monitor*, the first encounter between ironclads, ships covered with thick iron plate.

In his mind's eye, Mr. Huntington saw the great age of the 1880's, when mighty five-masters cruised up the Bay from distant ports to Baltimore, when sails of a thousand oyster boats whitened the Chesapeake skies and fifteen million bushels of oysters were harvested, and when showboats brought fun and frolic to the Tidewater towns.

There were still working sailboats on the Bay in Mr. Huntington's time, but he looked into the future and saw them vanishing in the mechanical age. He became convinced that some of them should be preserved so that young people could always appreciate the heritage of Tidewater adventure.

Mr. Huntington established the Mariners' Museum in order "to advance learning, the arts and sciences relating to or bearing on water-craft, the marine and marine navigation, thus to promote the public welfare." He directed that every aspect of ships and the sea be covered in the rich and varied collection — paintings, prints, whaling harpoons, ship models, carved figureheads, flags and books from all over the world. There would also be a special Chesapeake Bay Exhibition to illustrate the history of the Newport News maritime area.

In the museum you can learn about the sloops and schooners of Chesapeake Bay, the Baltimore clippers known in ports the world over, and ships with odd names like the pungy, sharpie and bugeye — and the ram, a sturdy three-master. Then there is the log canoe, once the sleekest sailing craft on the Bay, which the watermen used in racing, one team against another. It was first made in the early days, when settlers found they could build a long boat of two or three logs.

Later they added sails and centerboards and had a racing craft. And finally there is the skipjack, the last of commercial sailing boats on Chesapeake Bay.

Today you might still see a graceful one-masted skipjack on the Bay, out among the rowboats, runabouts, cabin cruisers and commercial boats, where people fish for sport or to earn their livelihood, and sometimes both. This vast Bay has been called "the best fishing hole in America." One of the greatest fishermen of them all was Captain John Smith, who claimed to have taken in fifty-two sturgeon at one haul, and sixty-two at another. Fish were large in those days and the stories about them larger. The early settlers told of bringing in fish six, nine and even sixteen feet long!

From these waters come two hundred species of fish, in addition to crab, clam, oyster and terrapin. Fishermen bring in everything from catfish up the rivers (sometimes weighing twenty-five pounds) and snapping turtles to striped bass, perch, shad, channel bass, Norfolk spot, bluefish, flounder, sea robin and sharks.

Sometimes you can see the fishermen out with huge nets after the menhaden, or alewife. This funny little fish, related to the herring, is the most numerous in the ocean and is caught in great numbers, sometimes 500,000 in a net. Usually the Tidewater fisherman speaks of the size of his catch in terms of "boxes," with one hundred pounds of fish to a box. But they figure the menhaden by the millions. You've probably never eaten one, for they are mostly ground up to be used as oil in making soap and linoleum.

It's a wonderful world, a different world, the land of the Chesapeake Bay and the watermen. Until recent years the watermen were isolated and lived much as their fathers and grandfathers did. With highways, bridges and better communications, their ways are changing and becoming modern. Many of them find they no longer can earn a living by fishing. They must look for jobs in factories, but their hearts remain on the Bay.

The scenery changes in every cove and estuary. Up at Smith Point, for example, where the Maryland-Virginia boundary cuts across the Bay, you might spot nests of ospreys, or fish hawks, in the broken limbs of trees. Or even a bald eagle, one of the last of his kind, soaring above his high perch. Smith Point is just below the meeting ground of the Potomac River and the Bay — and that river can offer a surprise itself, by whipping up seven-foot waves in less than fifteen minutes.

Here the Bay is at its widest, twenty-two miles across to the Eastern Shore. Out in the middle the big northbound ocean-going liners continue on their heading to pass the Naval Academy at Annapolis on their way to Baltimore. The skippers of the pilot boats know the way so well, they can steer a straight course once inside the Virginia capes, changing only a few degrees all the way.

Just about the time they're abeam of Smith Point on the port side, Tangier Island is off the starboard. Tangier, a marshy wisp of land just above the tide, laced with little bridges across watery sluices, has a population of less than a thousand — expert watermen who depend on fishing, oystering and crabbing for their livelihood.

If you ever go there — and you can, on the mailboat from Crisfield, Maryland, on the Eastern Shore — you'll find the Tangier Island harbor thronged with picturesque fishing craft. Most of the skippers are skilled sons of the sea who represent a hardy way of life. In his Mariners' Museum, Archer M. Huntington gave them his respect and told a part of their story. Pungy, bugeye, ram, log canoe and skipjack may disappear — but the legends and lore of the Chesapeake Bay watermen will live forever.

Soft crab float, Tangier Island

Chapter 3

The Dark Ponds

Often I've wondered about the scene that greeted Virginia's first settlers. What was it really like? Is there any area like it still remaining?

"I know a place that will surprise you," said my friend, Frederick Huette. "Two places, if you are patient."

We were at the *Gardens-by-the-Sea* in Norfolk, one of the most beautiful spots in all Virginia, thanks largely to Mr. Huette's efforts as director. Thousands of plants and flowers are woven together by pathways and serpentine canals. And there's a special treat for youngsters aboard the mighty schooner *Hispaniola* which sails to high adventure on "Treasure Island."

Now, said he, there would be a special discovery for me.

The odd thing is that this distinguished botanist and horticulturist, who knows and loves Virginia, was not born here, but in France. Sometimes we who are native Virginians take our treasures too much for granted. Often it takes someone with a broader background to see these treasures in perspective and appreciate them fully.

19

Gardens-by-the-Sea

While we drove away from the Gardens, I recalled the story of how the voyagers from England aboard the three small ships dropped anchor off Cape Henry on April 26, 1607. A party went ashore, saw Indians and was met with an inhospitable flurry of arrows. They built a shallop, or small boat, and explored, observing spring flowers, tasting oysters, and eating strawberries four times as large as those they knew in England.

We stopped barely three miles from the place of that first landing. I was surprised.

"Yes, the scene here is much as it was when the English explored it. They may even have walked this way in those first days," said Mr. Huette. We were at the beginning of a wilderness footpath in Seashore State Park. "The swampy conditions have protected this virgin forest from fire and logging. This unique fragment of nature is the northernmost frontier of trees and plants you usually find in the Deep South — Louisiana, Florida, or Georgia. It is the meeting ground of southern swampland, coastal sand dune and northern forest."

So it was. Along the trail I observed that bald cypress are the most abundant trees. They cover about one-third of the wilderness park. Some of the large cypress trees, with massive "knees" growing up from the roots, are over five hundred years old. They are the oldest living things on the trail.

Other trees at the northern limit of their range are the low-spreading live oaks, water tupelos, red bays and American olive, or devilwood, with clusters of small yellow blossoms and olive-like fruits. Above the moist-soaked lowland, the vegetation changes. One unusually dry spot supports subtropical yucca plants and cactus. Then there are loblolly pines, the fast-growing, tall and straight tree of the coastal plain, with clusters of pale green needles. Nearby is the northern forest of spreading white oak, sweet gum and hickory, which was especially valuable to the early colonists. Den trees, usually hollow logs, are the homes of raccoons, fox and other small animals rarely seen by day.

We were quiet and luckily caught sight of a belted kingfisher, always a solitary traveler, fishing for his meal in one of the cypress pools. Pitted bark on pine trees showed where the shy sapsucker had dug through to feed on insects and tree sap.

"Now," Mr. Huette said, "to the Great Dismal — one of the wonders of the continent."

The Great Dismal Swamp! The legendary land of untamed wild beauty astride the Virginia and North Carolina border — where dense forests sprout from spongy peat ground, threaded by canals and ditches, many grown over like green tunnels untouched by sunlight. I could hardly wait to see the paradise for hunters, fishermen and plant lovers — a land that has never surrendered its mystery.

To get there, we drove south thirty miles from Norfolk. Almost at the edge of the road was the canal linking Deep Creek, Virginia, with Joyce Creek, North Carolina, twenty-two miles away. In 1787, when Patrick Henry was governor, it was decided to build the canal. Called the Dismal Swamp Ship Canal, it was dug by slave labor without benefit of machinery or explosives. It did not provide navigation for flat boats until 1805. It is now part of the famous inland waterway. In a sturdy boat you can follow this waterway all the way to Florida.

At one time the swamp covered 1500 square miles, but bulldozers and drainage canals have cut it down. Now it covers about 600 square miles.

The swamp took millions of years to form, as layers of marine fossils were laid down by the ocean waters extending inland as far as Richmond, Fredericksburg and Washington. This was once the ancient sea floor. Trees, flowers, and ferns have flourished in the swamp for millions of years.

At a crossroads called Wallaceton, we stopped to meet Captain Millard A. Dunn, one of the veteran trappers and guides who live on the fringes of the swamp — and they're all called Captain, or "Cap'n." We boarded his flat-bottom boat, no bigger than a rowboat, powered by an eighteen-horsepower motor, and headed up the side canal, or "feeder ditch," into the swamp. The captain sang to us the old ballad about the young Indian who lost his beloved:

> "They made her a grave too cold and damp
> For a soul so warm and true:
> And she's gone to the Lake of the Dismal Swamp,
> Where all night long, by a fire-fly lamp,
> She paddles her white canoe."

Dismal Swamp Canal

He cracked a wry smile. "This is the way we're going, y' know."

For miles the banks of the canal were lush and thick with tangled foliage, hollies loaded with berries, pale blue hepatica, Virginia bluebell, crepe myrtle, oleander and altheas, luxuriant and exotic plants arising from rich, humid soil.

An animal darted through the woods, too swift to identify. "No end of deer, bear and bobcat, 'coon, muskrat or quail, either," said the Cap'n. "A hunter's paradise, but when you get tracking through this swamp it's mighty hard to carry anything out. Life's easier on the bird watchers — they can see them by the thousands."

We entered Lake Drummond, the heart of the swamp. It is a vast body of water three miles wide and six miles long — the largest natural lake in the state. It was an eerie place with water the color of iced tea, darkened from the peat layers twelve to fourteen feet thick. Gnarled, mossy cypress trees looked to me as if they were ready to

Dismal Swamp

die but Cap'n Dunn said they hadn't really changed much in the last forty years. They were still struggling to survive, gaunt and tilted, hollowed at the base, as though standing on pilings.

Unfortunately, hunting cabins and shacks around the lakeshore spoiled the scenery. They were surrounded by litter of cans and empty bottles and all manner of garbage piled high. I realized this was no primeval place. Wonderful timber, including prize cypress, has been logged in the Great Dismal and replaced with scrubby hardwood trees. Once there was even a logging railroad operating in a part of the Dismal, where the ground was firm enough to support it.

We passed tangled rhododendron, miles of red bay and jungles of holly so thick no man could penetrate them. "There's what makes it dismal — yet wonderful, too," said Cap'n Dunn.

Colonel William Byrd II gave it the name of Dismal Swamp. In 1728, he led a band of surveyors to run a dividing line between the disputing colonies of Virginia and North Carolina. Colonel Byrd, lost and out of food, to say nothing of being attacked by yellow flies, chiggers and ticks, considered this land a "filthy bogg." Byrd was one of the foremost men of his time. He became President of the Governor's Council, kept one of the finest libraries in America, and owned 180,000 acres of land. His great house, Westover, remains a showplace of Virginia.

Presently we came to another canal linked with the western edge of the lake. This is the "Washington Ditch," a fascinating parcel of history. The young thirty-one-year-old adventurer, surveyor and land promoter, George Washington, made his first of seven trips to the Dismal in 1763. In contrast to Byrd, he considered it a "glorious paradise, abounding in wild fowls and game," an excellent opportunity for investment. He and others (including Patrick Henry) organized a lumber and land firm called the "Adventurers for Draining the Great Dismal Swamp." The company dug drainage ditches. This canal was an outlet for timber. No profit was made but the canal, the Washington Ditch, still exists — possibly as the oldest man-made waterway in North America.

Chapter 4

The Jamestown Path

I was standing on a high bluff above the James River, in the cool shadow of history, following the course of Virginia's first colonists toward their ultimate destiny.

A solitary gull soared and wheeled above the water. A slim-necked egret stepped lightly with bright yellow feet between whale bones and marl on the pale river beach. Partially visible, beyond a bend upstream, lay wooded Jamestown Island.

It was springtime when the English settlers first saw it. The Virginia woods were like a paradise, the ground "all flowing over with faire flowers of sundry colors and kindes, as though it had been in any Garden or Orchard in England." There were oysters and fish, berries and fruits, deer, bear, fox, otter, beaver and muskrat, many kinds of trees and vines hanging in great clusters.

Going on to Jamestown itself, I found the only structure that remains standing is the Old Church Tower, covered with ivy. Almost all the rest has vanished into time.

Jamestown Church

But not quite all.

The weathered gravestones in the churchyard around the tower tell many stories, of early Virginia leaders — Berkeley, Harrison, Ludwell and Lee — who are buried beneath them. So does the towering sycamore tree that has separated the grave of Reverend James Blair from the grave of his wife. Blair was one of the founders of the College of William and Mary.

Down at the river's edge, the "High Way" of crushed stone and shell and earth was the first street in English America. The "Back Streete" excavations made by archaeologists of the National Park Service reveal foundations of what they believe was an early apartment house.

Around the peninsula, overlooking the James River about a mile from the first settlement, the state has created a life-size replica of the original fort. It helps us to imagine how the settlers went about felling trees in the cool of spring and building their triangular palisaded defenses. They mounted cannons at the lookout posts in the corners. Inside the walls, they erected their first church, storehouse and homes, with hand-hewn beams and marsh reeds for thatching the roofs.

They cleared open spaces and planted wheat brought from home for next year's crop. June was a good month. The first church communion was celebrated. Relations with the Indians seemed to be promising. The territories of the Powhatan Confederacy, south of the Potomac River, included about thirty different tribes. In 1607, about 5000 Indians, of whom 1500 were warriors, lived within sixty miles of Jamestown itself.

The replica of the old fort is authentic, yet I like best to wander along the original foundations and the winding, shadowy paths of old Jamestown. They are serene and peaceful, filled with the feeling of oldness that links a modern generation with the spirit of the past.

At a secluded point overlooking the river, you can reflect on the adventures of the founding fathers, their good luck and their bad luck, and try to compare their actions with something that might happen today.

I think of the first explorations in the New World as being somewhat like the race today for a beachhead on the moon.

The French, Portuguese, Italians and Spanish had started for the New World first. The British followed, hoping to establish their own foothold of empire and cut into the monopoly of riches. They wanted their share of international prestige that would come from penetrating distant horizons.

The founding father of Virginia was Sir Walter Raleigh, an adventurous investor, who never saw this far country himself. He was licensed by the Crown to explore, settle and exploit a large portion of the new land. It sounded so attractive that the region was named in honor of the Virgin Queen Elizabeth. The name "Virginia" at first applied to the entire Atlantic Coast north of the Spanish settlements in Florida.

Between 1585 and 1602, Raleigh organized at least seven expeditions to Virginia, without a shilling of support from the Crown. All of them were doomed to failure. The most famous attempt was made in 1587 at Roanoke Island, on the coast of North Carolina, where the first English child, Virginia Dare, was born in the New World. That colony began well, but when a relief expedition came in 1590 not a trace of anyone could be found. Weeds sprouted about empty cabins; books and maps were strewn and moldering on the ground. It is possible that these settlers joined a band of nearby Indians, but the mystery of the "Lost Colony" has never been solved.

Despite Raleigh's failure, he inspired New World fever in the air of England. The old feudal system, in which a few lords controlled the land and people, was nearing its end. Industry was growing. England had defeated the Spanish Armada and was ready to flex its might and muscles anywhere on earth.

The public was told that Virginia would be settled for the glory of God, the honor of the King and the welfare of England. Of course, it was also for the benefit of the new Virginia Company, chartered by King James I to take up where Sir Walter Raleigh left off. If the wealthy shareholders of this firm could create a permanent settlement and tap the treasures of the New World, their profits would soar.

Aboard the three ships, the *Susan Constant, Discovery* and *Godspeed*, high-prowed, square-sailed little ships that tossed about the lonely, perilous sea for four months, was a varied group of men. Some dreamed of fame or fortune . . . of being rewarded with titles or land . . . of finding the Northwest Passage to the wealth of Asia. Among them were gentlemen of high position and some of humble birth. But they were the kind of men who would be ready to travel through outer space

29

Replicas of the Godspeed, Discovery *and* Susan Constant

and look for adventure on the surface of the moon if they lived today.

After they were settled at Jamestown, Captain Christopher Newport, the commander of the expedition, hoisted anchor and sailed for home. He carried a cargo of timber and sassafras, the first cash crops. He left behind one hundred five hopeful men, who eagerly waited for his return with reinforcements. They knew the most difficult problem was to maintain the long supply line from England.

Then came July and August, the humid summer. Food spoiled in the heat. The low, swampy land swarmed with mosquitoes. The settlers realized they had chosen a poor site. The brackish water proved dangerous for drinking. There were no preventives, no cures and little knowledge of the dread diseases — malaria, typhoid and dysentery.

By the end of September, fifty men had perished. Starvation and homesickness were constant companions of the survivors, all inexperienced in wilderness living. They bickered and did little. The seven members of the resident council appointed by the Virginia Company could not provide leadership, for they were feuding among themselves.

At the water's edge stands a statue of the man who emerged as the dominant personality of the colony. He faces the river as a heroic bearded figure with long hair and flowing cape, his hand fixed at the sword in his scabbard. This was Captain John Smith, who possessed rare courage and a will to survive. He became a legendary personality of early American history. "Captain Smith," wrote Thomas Jefferson, "next to Sir Walter Raleigh may be considered as the founder of our colony."

John Smith was a strange fellow, rough-cut, the son of a tenant farmer, who had been imprisoned as a troublemaker on the journey from England. He was arrogant, but he was also a man of tremendous physical and moral endurance, who was honest, brave, sensible and well informed.

Possibly Smith saved the colony by employing the famous saying attributed to him, "He who will not work shall not eat." He took firm control. He rationed the slender food supply and made everyone work. He made friends with the Indians, particularly with Chief Powhatan, obtaining food when famine threatened.

The most legendary encounter of Smith's exciting career happened in December, when he was captured by Indians and nearly slain. But the fair Pocahontas stepped between him and his executioners and convinced her father, the chief, to spare the Englishman's life. We have only Smith's word about this episode. But once you accept Captain Smith as the dashing adventurer, the skilled mapmaker and the writer of historical works that have endured to this day, then anything in his colorful reports becomes believable.

New settlers arrived. Some of the first pioneers returned to England. In 1609, John Smith was forced by a serious burn from an explosion of gunpowder to head for home. He would never again visit Virginia, though later he undertook several voyages to New England and did much to promote interest in America.

For Jamestown, that winter of 1609 became the "starving time." Epidemics broke out. Disorder and dissension rose anew. Disease, sickness, pestilence, famine and Indian arrows struck the colony at the shore of the James River. The settlers were reduced to eating rice, rats and roots. They became scavengers stalking the fields where we walk today. A handful sailed for England aboard the *Swallow*, fleeing the fate of death that claimed new lives every day.

Life grew so horrible that men were digging corpses out of the graves and stewing the meat with roots and herbs.

Finally the following May, when all seemed lost, Sir Thomas Gates arrived with a relief expedition. He was astounded to find only sixty-five settlers still living, and they only barely so. Jamestown was a graveyard. Most of the settlers insisted on leaving their nightmarish village for the comforts and security of their homeland.

The great Virginia experiment seemed at an end. In June, 1610, the colonists boarded the ships, bade Jamestown a farewell without sorrow and headed down the James River toward the open sea. But as they were about to leave the Bay, they met the fleet of Lord de la Warre, sent by the Virginia Company. With him were one hundred fifty new settlers and provisions. He turned the colonists back to Jamestown, whether they wanted to go or not. Soon they were surprised to find they were not only surviving, but prospering. The settlers planted squash, beans and corn in terraced hills, in the Indian fashion. The harvests were bountiful, and the fear of famine disappeared. Under the stern hand of de la Warre and his successor, Sir Thomas Dale, known as the "Iron Governor," the newcomers began to spread, pushing inland to better locations. Dale divided the common fields and made every man a landowner, forcing the lazy to work or starve.

As more and more people came to Virginia, other towns were built. Kecoughtan, pronounced Keck-o-tan (at Hampton-Newport News), became a permanent settlement. Henricus (or Henrico) was boldly established well up the James River. Then came Charles City (first called Bermuda Hundred). Together with Jamestown, these would become known as the "Four Ancient Boroughs," the only ones established directly under the Virginia Company, before the Crown decided to claim control of the colony.

Jamestown now lay in the center of an expanding province. It was an incredible victory over ignorance, bad luck, bitter argument and broken promises from home. During the first fifteen years 14,000 settlers were sent from England. Of that number 13,000 were doomed to perish. Still the colony took root.

The little church tower, the only surviving ruin of the original James-town, was not begun until about 1639. It was constructed of brick, an advanced material for these early years. The walls are three feet thick and have been standing more than three hundred years.

Walk inside the Memorial Church, adjoining the tower. There are cobblestones on the ground, crude but sturdy, even older than the brick. They are believed to be part of the foundation of a church that stood on this spot in 1619.

That year, 1619, saw lively activity at Jamestown.

A boatload of one hundred "young, handsome and honestly edu-cated maids" arrived at a time when only a few married couples but many bachelors made up the colony. Presently all were wed after whirlwind courtships.

The population of the colony was less than 2500, yet it was thriving on the new tobacco trade. Other industries had been started with vary-ing degrees of success. Lumbering, the fur trade, a glass works, and even an attempt to cultivate silkworms for a silk industry had been tried. Then it was discovered that Virginia soil was ideal for tobacco. John Rolfe, who married Princess Pocahontas in the earliest Jamestown church and built a home for her at the Henrico settlement, is credited with the first experiments. In 1612 or 1613 he planted tobacco seeds from the West Indies and grew the leaf that proved as fine and fragrant "as any under the sun." Within a few years, the demand for Virginia tobacco was so great overseas that it was grown everywhere, on the streets and even between graves. It shaped the fate of the people. It would make some men rich and others slaves. It would provide the wealth to construct elegant mansions, and yet weaken the fertility of the soil of Virginia. To grow tobacco, open fields and endless supplies of new, fertile soil were needed. This led to a scattering of population on plantations, rather than a concentration in cities.

In 1619 the first Negroes from Africa arrived at Jamestown aboard a Dutch slave vessel. Members of that first group were sold as indentured servants, who could and did earn their freedom. It would be more than a generation before the practice of slavery was firmly established.

In late July, 1619, the first representative assembly convened hopefully in the church at Jamestown. It offered a precedent for the same

Arrival of Negroes at Jamestown

kind of self-government in British colonies that Englishmen enjoyed at home. Eleven districts, called plantations, sent two spokesmen each into the church with the cobblestone foundations. They enacted simple laws to govern the colonists' behavior. It was the beginning of the legislative process in America that evolved into the present-day General Assembly of Virginia, and served as the base for our national system of democratic lawmaking.

Jamestown served well as capital of the young colony. Land and opportunity were plentiful. New settlers arrived, filled with hope and dreams. Some came to toil in the fields — bounded to servitude. If a prospective settler was unable to raise his passage money from England, he could engage himself to a master for a period of five or seven years and have the expenses paid for him. A few indentured servants were criminals, whose sentences had been commuted to deportation. The servant was required to work without wages, but at the end of his time he was free. Then he too could obtain a modest grant of land and begin for himself a life of promise as an independent yeoman farmer.

There were Indian wars and royal governors who held power in their hands, but still the colony prospered and grew. In 1633, a new settlement named Middle Plantation was established inland. It was later renamed Williamsburg. Two free schools were established for children, both near the town of Hampton. An effort was made to establish a college at Henrico. Construction of buildings improved and houses became more comfortable. Memorial Church was erected and must have been considered by all a sign of Jamestown's prosperity and permanence.

This was a settlement dominated by small, industrious, liberty-loving farmers. Their estates did not, as a rule, exceed one or two thousand acres. Property owners were the merchants, yeoman, carpenters, and joiners of crowded, bustling Jamestown, as well as the outlying tobacco farmers. They were Englishmen stoutly loyal to the English sovereign. When Charles II regained the throne after the civil war with Oliver Cromwell, he affectionately called the colony his "Old Dominion," which ever since has been more than a nickname, really a second name for Virginia.

But the Virginians were also becoming increasingly conscious of their strength and jealous of their rights. Under the administration of

35

Sir William Berkeley, feeling mounted to the pitch of open rebellion. The settlers resented his highhanded acts and lack of concern for the small planter. They demanded protection from the Indians who often raided the settlements west of Jamestown. In the winter of 1675 parties of Indians and whites committed murders and atrocities against each other. Five chieftains of the Susquehannocs were maliciously slain under a flag of truce on the Maryland side of the Potomac River. Their followers fled over the frozen river, striking at the plantation of young Nathaniel Bacon on the James River.

Many interpretations have been placed on the exciting episode known as Bacon's Rebellion. Bacon organized a force of frontiersmen and went after the Indians. He marched into Jamestown itself, forcing Berkeley to flee for his life and burning almost everything in town, including the church and the state house.

Bacon became violently ill with malaria soon after. He died in October, 1676, and the rebellion collapsed. Berkeley came out of exile on the Eastern Shore and ordered the execution of all of Bacon's band. The hot-tempered Bacon was destined to become, rightly or wrongly, a colorful figure of history.

The town was rebuilt but never quite recovered. After another fire in 1698, it was decided to move rather than rebuild the capital. It is unlikely that anyone mourned departing the cluttered town surrounded by brackish, disease-breeding swamps.

Its mission had been accomplished. It had seen Virginia grow into a colony of great extent, with a population of about 80,000. By the time of the American Revolution, it had faded away completely as a town.

The ruins were left to the ravages of time and the river.

In 1893, a group of citizens organized as the Association for the Preservation of Virginia Antiquities undertook to save what they could of the old townsite. They felt it was a national treasure that should not be allowed to perish altogether. They raised enough money to purchase the Old Church Tower, the graveyard and the west end of the town. Later the National Park Service undertook to study, save and properly interpret the major portion of the ruins.

Today we are able to walk in the Jamestown path and to imagine all that happened here over three hundred years ago.

Chapter 5

Discovery at Williamsburg

What is Williamsburg today?

Sometimes it is said to be an old, old town. A museum of the past.

Whenever I go there I always find something new, or learn something new. Even about the past. History changes as we discover new reasons for the actions of men long ago.

Imagine how the archaeologists felt when they excavated the grounds of the Governor's Palace in 1927. They came across rows of buried men. Who were they? Why were they here? How many rows would they discover?

They kept digging, carefully, until they found eleven rows, containing the bodies of one hundred fifty-six men and two women. They could identify the men as Revolutionary soldiers who died during the battle of Yorktown, when the Palace was used as a military hospital. The women were thought to have been nurses, but no one could say for sure. Their exact identity remains one of those surviving mysteries of the past.

Bruton Parish Church

When I visit Williamsburg, I think of a minister who lived there and helped rediscover it. It was in the days when Williamsburg was "lost" to history. This minister was Dr. William A. R. Goodwin.

Dr. Goodwin first came to Williamsburg in 1902 after attending the Virginia Theological Seminary in Alexandria. He found the little town dilapidated and run down. After 1780, when the capital was moved to Richmond, Williamsburg had stepped backward in importance. It had not quite died, as Jamestown had, but it was like a bear cub in hibernation.

The Capitol building was gone, burned in a fire long ago. However, the site and original foundations were being preserved faithfully by the Association for the Preservation of Virginia Antiquities. The Governor's Palace was gone, too. A public school stood on the land it had occupied.

The College of William and Mary was open, but as a shadow of its former self. It was so poor the state was forced to take it over in 1906.

The state of Bruton Parish Church was particularly bad. When Dr. Goodwin thought of the part it once played in Virginia life, and how it should have been cared for as a fine example of a colonial church, its present condition saddened him. The walls and windows were the originals, but the inside, including the pews and pulpit, were badly damaged and disfigured. At once, he drew up plans to restore the church to its earlier appearance.

Few people in Virginia seemed to care, but Dr. Goodwin was determined. He was a man with imagination and he stirred others to action. King Edward VII of Great Britain sent a historic Bible. President Theodore Roosevelt gave a lectern. J. Pierpont Morgan, one of the world's richest men, helped also. These people far from Tidewater Virginia recognized the importance of Bruton Parish Church and wanted to see it restored.

Though he was transferred away, Dr. Goodwin never forgot that experience. In 1926, he was moved back to Bruton Parish.

Williamsburg was, thought Dr. Goodwin, the most interesting place in America. He remembered those who had lived there before and the things they had done. He was determined that not just a few buildings but the whole town should be restored.

Dr. Goodwin brought his vision to Mr. John D. Rockefeller, Jr., a wealthy man who loved beauty in all its forms. Mr. Rockefeller listened carefully. He came to Williamsburg and together with Dr. Goodwin walked the old streets. In place of the cheap amusement halls, filling stations and restaurants, they saw the past renewed as large as life, not as a museum but as a place to spark the future with ideas and ideals worthy of the old "golden age."

These two were gifted men. They dared to dream. They believed that history was not dull and lifeless, but alive with ideas of the past that still live today.

They could picture the panorama of time.

They saw the year of 1699 when the capital came to Williamsburg, named in honor of King William III. Its location on a high ridge between the York and James Rivers, free of the uncomfortable dampness of Jamestown was especially in its favor. It already had a brick church, Bruton Parish. Clustered around it were several stores and houses, two mills, a smith's shop, and a lodging house.

The town had a new college, too, called the College of William and

The College of William and Mary

The Colonial Capitol

Mary. The only other college in the colonies was Harvard, in Massachusetts. If this college lasted, the rich planters could send their sons to study here rather than to the universities in England.

The royal governor, Francis Nicholson, was proud of Williamsburg. He laid out the streets and open squares, with a wide central avenue named for the Duke of Gloucester. The avenue joined the College of William and Mary at one end with the new Capitol building at the other.

His plan was extraordinary. Unlike most cities of today, where houses and people are jammed closely together, he directed that each house should have sufficient space around it for a garden and orchard.

Williamsburg grew and prospered. It was the capital of the largest and most heavily populated of all British colonies. Virginia territory stretched far to the west, as far west as man dared dream. The political power of Williamsburg over this vast domain was expressed in the

41

great Capitol building. The prestige of the Crown was there for all to see in the Governor's Palace, completed about 1720. These elegant brick buildings were a far cry from the old rough-hewn shelters at Jamestown.

Every person in Virginia was subject to the government at Williamsburg. There were the large planters of Tidewater and the tenants on Lord Fairfax's baronial estate of five million acres on the Northern Neck. There were the merchants and dockhands at the busy wharves of Yorktown, and the freeholders of the Piedmont, the foothills of the Appalachian Mountains, building their water-powered gristmills and new villages. There were German settlers and the Scotch-Irish, land-hungry and freedom-hungry, moving down from Pennsylvania into the Valley of Virginia. And there were the adventure-craving frontiersmen and agents of land speculators deep in Indian territory, the "wild west" of that day.

Williamsburg was a cultured place, the planters' capital. Luxuries

such as fine carriages, wines, silver plate, books and paintings came from tobacco profits. Some of the planters lived in the rolling Piedmont, but most leaders of this landed aristocracy came from the Tidewater. They had their mansions on the plantations, but they spent many weeks of the year in Williamsburg.

It was an exciting and important period in the history of Virginia — and in the history of the whole world.

But despite prosperity, this was not democracy's hour. The Indians were pushed to the West or destroyed. The slave trade flourished. Many indentured servants worked hard for their living. By today's standards, it was a crude existence. The average man received little formal education. Boys were often apprenticed to a trade with little opportunity for an education.

On the plantations, the aristocracy was trained to leadership from youth, to serve as lawmakers in Williamsburg, as justices of the peace, and as vestrymen of their own parish. Barely one hundred families

Duke of Gloucester Street

dominated the productive economy, its political offices and its social life.

But as Virginia and the other colonies matured, a wave of new feeling grew. In 1765, Patrick Henry, who was not an aristocrat but a struggling frontier lawyer, stood in the House of Burgesses to denounce the Stamp Act, which placed a tax on all legal documents, academic degrees and licenses issued in the colonies. Henry claimed that only the legislatures of the colonies had the right to tax the American people.

The British royal governors had much cause for concern at Williamsburg. One of them, Lord Botetourt, became so upset when the Assembly dared to protest against the British Revenue Act in 1769 that he ordered the burgesses to dissolve and leave Williamsburg. But they proceeded in a body to Raleigh Tavern and indignantly drew up a boycott of British goods.

The last royal governor, John Murray, fourth Earl of Dunmore, arrived in a hopeful frame of mind in 1771. But it was not to continue long. Two years later he was angered by the efforts of Virginians to unite the colonies in the growing dispute with England. This began when five patriots (Thomas Jefferson, Dabney Carr, Patrick Henry and the talented brothers Richard Henry Lee and Francis Lightfoot Lee) gathered secretly at Raleigh Tavern to organize Virginia's Committee of Correspondence. When rebellious talk spread through the General Assembly, the governor gave the same order as his predecessor, "Go home. Your meeting is over!" And they went.

But freedom was in the air.

When the General Assembly convened at the Capitol in 1774, the shocking news was received of punishment inflicted by the English on the city of Boston for the "tea party" protest against taxation from abroad. The Virginia burgesses voted to stop all trade with England until colonial grievances were adjusted. As "representatives of the people," they decided to issue a call for an open meeting with leaders of other colonies. That meeting would be known as the First Continental Congress.

The Virginians still pledged their loyalty, provided the Crown did not interfere with their rights, liberties and properties. But Patrick Henry felt that fighting was near and urged the militiamen to keep their powder dry and rifles ready. "Is life so dear, or peace so sweet," he demanded in his boldest words, spoken in Richmond in early 1775, "as to be purchased at the expense of chains and slavery? Forbid it, Almighty God! I know not what course others may take, but as for me, give me liberty or give me death."

Governor Dunmore grew desperate and frightened. He stationed British marines at the Palace to protect his family, but then he blundered badly. On the night of April 21, 1775, he sent a squad of marines to break into the Magazine, the brick arsenal standing in the green expanse of Market Square. They stole the powder and carried it to an English ship in the York River.

The people were furious. That supply of powder was for their defense, by their militia. Troops began to muster in various places. Patrick Henry led a party of armed volunteers from Hanover County marching on the capital.

But something even more decisive was brewing. Less than forty-eight hours before the removal of the powder, the British had fired on Massachusetts militiamen at Lexington. Soon after, at Concord the shot was fired that was "heard around the world."

When this news reached Williamsburg, the *Virginia Gazette* printed an extra. "The sword is now drawn," wrote the editor. "God knows when it will be sheathed."

For Dunmore it was time to beat a hasty retreat. The last of the seven royal governors to live in the elegant Governor's Palace fled to Norfolk before dawn one June morning to fight on for his cause. Thus for all time British rule in Virginia ended.

The first governor of the new commonwealth arrived to take residence in the Palace. It was the man of the people, Patrick Henry himself, who demonstrated his faith in democracy by starting the practice of calling the voters "fellow citizens." He was succeeded by Thomas Jefferson, who served during the darkest hours of the Revolution, when the capital was removed in 1780 to safer ground at Richmond.

From then on, Williamsburg stepped backstage in history, into the dim shadows of its own past.

But Dr. Goodwin and Mr. Rockefeller saw the ancient scenes of Henry and Jefferson, of Washington and Mason and Wythe coming

Palace of the Royal Governors

into and going out of the old houses and the Capitol building. They recalled the debates, discussions, the contributions to freedom these men and others made here. It was not only his money that Mr. Rockefeller considered contributing, but also his ideas. Where stood shattered foundations of buildings long gone from the scene, he saw a new city rising in the image of the old.

Thus, he agreed to contribute his money. The restoration would begin.

Architects were set to work on hundreds and thousands of sketches. Research experts were sent to study history in libraries, county courts and newspapers. They checked insurance records, diaries, old wills, almost any kind of evidence that would shed light on the city's past. Archaeologists began digging around foundations and sifting through the soil.

Educators, gardeners, artists and many kinds of experts were asked to participate in piecing together the lost secrets.

They found that over eighty of the original buildings were still standing.

Over the years almost five hundred buildings have been restored or reconstructed. Many of the unsightly filling stations and other out-of-place structures have been removed. This is the Williamsburg we see today, the capital of Virginia in its golden age brought back to life.

A friend of mine who works and lives at Williamsburg once showed me some amusing sights. "We have all the modern conveniences," he told me. "But we hide them." Telephone and electric wires are buried underground. His television antenna was hidden in the trees and the fire hydrant was surrounded by bushes so you couldn't see it. "Now look at the key to my front door." He reached for the inside pocket of his jacket and came out with a heavy iron key about eight inches long. "It is not the easiest item to carry around. But it's not easy to lose either."

Chapter 6

Fateful Friday at Yorktown

Yorktown was an old town, built on the cliffs of the York River, when the American Revolution came to its doorstep.

Today, together with Jamestown and Williamsburg, it is part of the "Triple Shrine" of the Virginia Peninsula.

It grew and prospered because of the rich tobacco trade passing through its harbor and warehouses. A number of fine homes were built by wealthy merchant families. Anyone visiting Yorktown can see that it still has much of the character of the long-vanished period, even though it started to decline before the Revolution when Tidewater tobacco lost its value.

On the level fields outside the quiet colonial "Town of York," the last decisive battle of the American Revolution was fought, ending almost seven years of struggle. The scene of war had stretched from Florida to Quebec, from the Atlantic Coast to the Wabash River in the far "Northwest" of that day. But through one of those odd turns of fate, this final masterstroke was to take place just twenty-three miles

Yorktown

from Jamestown. A good rider, with a fast horse, could cover that distance easily in a day.

Lieutenant General Earl Charles Cornwallis had entered Virginia with his British army in that spring of 1781. If he could conquer the Old Dominion, he believed the southern states "would fall without much difficulty."

He knew that Virginia fighting men were tough. He had met them before. They had been to the far-flung fronts. They were rugged, the Virginia mountain boys. Not much for fancy uniforms. They traveled light, usually wearing a buckskin hunting shirt and wide-brimmed hat. Each was equipped with knapsack, blanket, tomahawk, scalping knife and his trusted hunting rifle.

One of their leaders was George Rogers Clark, the young redheaded colonel, who led a little army of frontiersmen, the "Long Knives," against the British in the West. Another was General Andrew Lewis. His father, John Lewis, had come from Ireland after killing a lord in an argument over rents. He was a pioneer in settling the town of Staunton and furnished five sons to the Revolution. Colonel William Campbell, of Aspenvale, in southwestern Virginia, had led the Virginians down the narrow Indian trails to Kings Mountain, South Carolina, where, in October, 1780, they had fought Indian style and inflicted a bitter defeat on British troops in Cornwallis' command.

Colonel Daniel Morgan, of Winchester, was a fearless mountain man always to be found where action was the hottest. Cornwallis knew him *too* well. At Cowpens, South Carolina, in January, 1781, Morgan and his riflemen had scored a smashing victory over the British. After that, the British general began to pursue Morgan northward, eager to avenge the defeat. He followed Morgan to the southern border of Virginia.

On entering Virginia, Cornwallis had decided to break the back of Virginia's resistance. At first, the British moved up and down the state almost at will.

Benedict Arnold, the American who was a traitor to his country, tried to move from Portsmouth to capture Richmond. Heading a small British force, he sailed up the James River, landed at Westover, and inflicted a cruel raid on the city at the Falls of the James. Finally, he was repelled.

50

Cornwallis himself struck as far north as Culpeper, with a force of more than 5000. He was in pursuit of Continentals headed by the Marquis de Lafayette. But "Mad Anthony" Wayne arrived with a force from Pennsylvania to bolster Lafayette.

Now Cornwallis turned to the coast, through Richmond and Williamsburg, expecting to rendezvous with the British fleet. He chose Yorktown for his base and transferred the entire army of 7,500 there early in August.

Events moved swiftly once Cornwallis established his base. The news reached General Washington, who was at the head of his army outside New York. At once his eyes turned south, toward his native state. He decided to concentrate all forces on the capture of Cornwallis.

On reaching Williamsburg, Washington was made welcome to establish his headquarters in the large brick house of George Wythe on the Palace Green. The Commander-in-Chief spread his maps and charts. He dispatched appeals for reinforcements, blankets, bread, clothing, ammunition, horses and rum for his troops.

At sea, Washington's naval ally, Admiral François de Grasse, blockaded the mouth of Chesapeake Bay with a powerful squadron. Then, Lieutenant General Jean de Rochambeau arrived with his army from Rhode Island. Count Rochambeau set up headquarters at the home of Peyton Randolph on Nicholson Street, one block across the Green from Washington's quarters.

Soldiers were everywhere, bivouacked in the fields and meadows, waiting and wondering. Communications were much slower then. But de Grasse with his great flotilla offshore had the Bay sealed up tight as a drum, despite challenge after challenge from the British fleet.

On September 28 the hour was right. The mighty host of 16,000 tough, battle-trained American and French soldiers marched down the Peninsula toward Yorktown. They moved their batteries into a semicircle around the English lines. That night Washington slept with his troops. Many times you read about his being the guest in elegant mansions, but he was equally at home outdoors on the hard ground, in the company of humble men.

In October the barrage opened, with seventy French and American cannons hitting the British positions. At Yorktown today you can see a cannonball still embedded in a wall of the Nelson House, where Cornwallis had his headquarters.

51

The siege lasted three weeks. On the cool evening of October 14, American infantrymen made a dramatic and heroic thrust at one of the key outlying earth forts of the British called Redoubt 9. They captured it. A young lieutenant colonel named Alexander Hamilton led another four hundred men in hand-to-hand fighting at Redoubt 10. They captured it, too.

After that, Cornwallis knew it was over. He and his men had fought bravely as long as they could. The morning of October 17, he sent out a flag of truce. On October 18, at old Moore House, which you can still see on the Yorktown battlefield just behind the American lines, officers of both sides met to draft the surrender terms. The entire grounds are yours to study, for they are part of the Colonial National Historical Park.

Picture the scene at the hour of 2 P.M. on the fateful Friday, October 19, 1781. A great crowd gathered on the open field to witness the ceremony. The French troops were drawn up in their finest uniforms, in a formation one mile long. Facing them was another formation equally long — the Americans, as neat and proud as they had ever been, filled with memories of the dark, ragged, hungry, hopeless hours behind them. Washington and Rochambeau were at the head of the troops.

Surrender at Yorktown

They were mounted on handsome, spirited horses.

The British Army marched out from Yorktown between the French and American armies to lay down their arms. Washington, though by nature a man of generosity and good will, refused to allow the English to fly their Union Jack. He could not forget how the Americans had not been allowed to fly their Stars and Stripes when they had to surrender Charleston, South Carolina. Nor would he receive the sword that Cornwallis sent to him. Instead, he directed that it be given to General Benjamin Lincoln, the American commander at the fall of Charleston. General Lincoln kept his hands on the reins of his horse while he looked at the sword being held out to him by a British officer. He felt that the sword should not be his any more than Washington's. He respected the British fighting men and their leaders. Perhaps the time might come when British and American would stand again shoulder to shoulder in a future common cause. He asked that the sword be restored to General Cornwallis.

After the soldiers stacked their colors and arms, the drums rolled and the British band broke into the tune of an old march, "The World Turned Upside Down." Off marched the British brigades. The world *had* turned upside down for them.

Chapter 7

On to Richmond

When I visit Richmond, I feel how old — no, not old, but how *continuous* — this state of Virginia really is. More than any other place, the capital city speaks for the entire state, of its newness as well as its age, of the wide diversity of its people, of their many interests and their hopes. It binds us together, past, present and future.

I have been all over this country and all over the world, and experienced the thrill of walking down the streets of great cities — London, Paris, Cairo, Tokyo, San Francisco and New York. There is some little something of them all in Richmond, and a little something else besides. I have walked in Richmond alongside visitors from another country and watched them. They felt it, too.

The location of the capital city at the Falls of the James River reminds me of the topographic diversity of the state. Heading upstream from the Tidewater, or coastal plain, a barrier of higher, harder rock marks the approach to an inland region of Virginia. The barrier is called the Fall Line, a name soundly chosen.

Virginia State Capitol

The Great Falls, in the north, are a natural wonder of the Potomac River you would scarcely expect to find at the back door of Washington, D.C. The river splashes over upthrust towering boulders and leaps through thundering cataracts with the fury of a storm at sea. Farther south, at Fredericksburg, you encounter the Falls of the Rappahannock. Stretch a line still farther and it will be dampened by the Falls of the James at Richmond and the Falls of the Appomattox at Petersburg.

Step over the line and enter the section of the state called Piedmont, derived from two French words, *pied* (for foot) and *mont* (for mountain).

About the Falls of the James and the country surrounding them: "The water is as clear as crystal and as sweet as milk," once wrote William Byrd II, the founder of Richmond. "It is a fine place for Cattle and Hoggs, for Sheep and Goats, and fortunately there is a large creature of the Beef kind, but much larger, called a Buffalo, which may be bred up tame and is good both for food and labour. In a word, there is nothing so deserving of the name I have given it of the Land of Eden."

The Virginia Capitol, rising above the trees on the hill, is one of the finest buildings in America. That able architect, Thomas Jefferson, created it, with the typical Jeffersonian dome. He found his inspiration in the southern part of France at a village called Nimes, where the Romans had constructed a beautiful temple, the Maison Carrée, two thousand years ago. Scores of impressive public buildings in the United States have since been influenced by his design.

Inside the building, a statue of George Washington stands in the rotunda as tall and erect as Washington himself. It is the only statue of Washington made during his lifetime, and is Virginia's most priceless art treasure.

Surrounding Washington in the rotunda are marble busts of the other seven Presidents born in Virginia — Jefferson, Madison, Monroe, William Henry Harrison, John Tyler, Zachary Taylor and Woodrow Wilson; and a bust of the Marquis de Lafayette, the young French hero.

The little central portion of the building is filled with memories. In the old House of Delegates, Aaron Burr was tried for treason in 1807. Robert E. Lee here accepted command of the Virginia troops during the Civil War. The Confederate Congress met from 1862 until the end of the war.

The political pot still boils around Capitol Square. This is what makes it most exciting, especially when the General Assembly is in session, every other year. The talk is serious — in whispers, mumbles and oratory — in the hotel lobbies, restaurants, the Capitol corridors, and in the House and Senate wings where laws are passed.

The lawmakers have the problems of today and tomorrow on their minds. They come from the Bay and the Eastern Shore and are concerned about crops of oysters, crabs and fish. They come from Norfolk, Newport News, Roanoke and northern Virginia — the urban centers — and worry about filling the needs of their booming population. They come from farm country and do not want their people left behind. The fate of Virginia's future is in their hands. They must decide important questions.

These lawmakers are watched and questioned by newspaper, radio and television reporters, who provide the means of answering directly to the people. They are visited by representatives of special interests and industries who want to keep the legislators informed, if not to influence their votes.

I remember the heavy pressure brought by representatives, or lobbyists, of the outdoor advertising industry — the billboards — to prevent the General Assembly from controlling the number of commercial signs along Virginia's highways. The debate went on in public, and the hush-hush in private. How would the vote go?

The billboard men were beaten! There are still too many signs on our roadsides, but the General Assembly was determined to do its duty to save the beauty of Virginia. The great men who sat in the Capitol many years ago would have been proud.

One day I received a telephone call from the United States Department of Commerce in Washington, D.C. Would I go to Richmond for a special assignment? "We want you to observe and report how visitors from overseas are welcomed and treated, and what they really think of that city," a government official told me. I leaped at the chance.

In Richmond, I went around with a group of English visitors under the guidance of the Richmond International Council, a group of volun-

St. John's Church

teer families who have entertained people from all over the world —
students, military personnel, businessmen, tourists.

We ate Smithfield ham and beaten biscuits. The English visitors
loved them. We stopped at white-framed St. John's Episcopal Church,
where Washington, Jefferson, Richard Henry Lee and other members
of the Virginia Convention heard the fiery Patrick Henry make his
immortal declaration of "Liberty or Death." In the area around St.
John's on Church Hill, the old houses were being renovated and lived
in.

"It reminds me of the little places at home," said an Englishman.
"Not as old, of course, but I'm surprised to find the Americans doing
this well in making their old treasures serve a useful purpose in a
modern age."

I was surprised, too. These visitors had been to New York, Niagara

Falls, Boston and Washington, yet they seemed overwhelmed in our Richmond. It was not only the sights they saw. It was also the genuine hospitality they received.

I have my special favorite spots in Richmond. One is the Museum of Fine Arts, not only because it offers one of the best art collections of the South, but also because it brings art to people all over the state through rolling galleries and artmobiles — a wonderful link between Richmond and all corners of Virginia.

Another favorite is Monument Avenue, lined with towering statues of Southern heroes, bordered with trees and fine old houses. Somehow, this broad boulevard has the touch of sorrow, pride and dignity, all in one.

An English couple and I drove out Monument Avenue to the trim, modern home of our host and hostess for the evening. These people often entertained guests from foreign countries through the Richmond International Council and they loved it. During the evening the lady of the house showed us her scrapbook and letters from many visitors. I noted one from far-off India, which read, "We never felt strangers in Richmond, which became a home away from home to us."

Monument Avenue

Chapter 8

The Legacy of George Mason

Gunston Hall is one of the greatest of the eighteenth-century mansions along the Potomac. It has an unforgettable setting, high above the wide, winding river. It has lovely gardens, of tall boxwood carefully trimmed and tended, and of holly brilliant with red berries. The house is a masterpiece of design and craftsmanship, executed by an amazing indentured servant named William Buckland, who created, with crude hand tools, woodwork of a beauty that machines cannot duplicate.

It has all of these, plus the memory of its master, George Mason.

Sometimes I fear that the physical substances before our eyes, the view, the garden and the house, obscure the deeper meaning of Gunston Hall as a shrine to George Mason, a philosopher of freedom. Buckland was the architect of his house, but Mason was the architect of a code of beliefs that enrich our America.

George Washington, Thomas Jefferson, James Madison, John Marshall, Patrick Henry — and Mason — leaders of the Revolution and shapers of the Union, have been called the "Great Generation." Though

Gunston Hall

he never held high public office, as the others did, George Mason surely belongs in this galaxy.

Mason's mind ran to large designs and broad principles. He was not one to "go along with the crowd" if he thought their ideas were wrong. His judgments generally proved correct, although decades often passed before they were fully appreciated. His objections to the Constitution of the United States were recognized through the adoption of the Bill of Rights. But George Mason's greatest contribution was in the field of human morality: he stood with Patrick Henry, Thomas Jefferson and George Washington for emancipation and education of the Negroes. He opposed the spread of slavery to the western states.

As Jefferson said, Mason was "one of those very rare intellects which are created only by a special effort of nature."

George Mason is today the least remembered and least understood of the famous men produced by Virginia during her "golden age." Outside the state his is a name only occasionally recognized, although his Virginia Declaration has been influential in all free nations of the world. Within Virginia, he and his career are known only a little better.

In mid-May, 1776, George Mason rode into Williamsburg. He had already written the Fairfax Resolves, a set of resolutions adopted by leaders of his county in July, 1774. They clearly defined the rights of the colonies against unjust, tyrannical abuses. The Resolves proposed a "firm union" of the colonies to solve their problems.

Now he had been appointed to the committee to draft the Declaration of Rights and the Constitution of the state. He was not the sort of man to push himself. Nor was he an orator with the magnetism of Patrick Henry. He was a deliberate thinker about individual liberty and the rights of man. No doubt that was why he was chosen to help prepare the drafts.

To help? He was *the* author of the Virginia Declaration of Rights. The Committee accepted with hardly a change his draft as the basis of the new government. The draft was unanimously adopted by the legislators assembled in the Capitol on June 15.

Next came the Constitution for the state. It, too, was mostly his work. It was the first written constitution of any state of the United States.

Then came the Declaration of Rights in 1776. It is known as the greatest single document produced at Williamsburg throughout its history. Starting in the spirit of the Fairfax Resolves, it proclaimed that:

"All men are by Nature equally free and independent, and have certain inherent rights, of which, when they enter into a State of Society, they cannot, by any Compact, deprive or divest their Posterity; namely, the Enjoyment of Life and Liberty, with the Means of acquiring and possessing Property, and pursuing Happiness and Safety."

In sixteen articles, the Mason Declaration set forth such fundamental rights as freedom of religion and the press; trial by jury; free elections; and the subordination of military to civil authority. Never in the world had there been anything like it. It was an outline for working democracy — and the outline still works.

Read over Mason's words. Then read the Declaration of Independence, drawn up one month later. You will find the wonderful document that begins, "We hold these truths to be self-evident . . ." is written in the language of Thomas Jefferson, but with the ideas of George Mason's Virginia Declaration of Rights.

The fundamental rights of man, of *all* men under the sight of their Creator, were Mason's concern. As a member of the Virginia House of Delegates from 1776 to 1788, he joined with Jefferson in the hard fight for religious freedom, and for separation of church and state. He was a delegate to the Constitutional Convention of 1787 in Philadelphia. But he refused to sign the Constitution because it failed to provide the abolition of slavery or sufficiently safeguard individual rights.

His objections to the Constitution contributed to the drafting of the first ten amendments to the Constitution, the Bill of Rights. The document was written by a man who had sat with him in preparing the Virginia Constitution, James Madison, a champion of freedom destined for glory.

George Mason wanted no honors. He refused appointment as a United States Senator, returning instead to the quiet of his own Gunston Hall.

The failure of Virginia to take a firm stand against slavery was a great disappointment to George Mason. Though he usually expressed

63

his thoughts in moderate terms, he became indignant at the thought that one man could buy and sell another. He denounced slavery as being "diabolical in itself and disgraceful to mankind."

"We came equals into this world," Mason said once to the Fairfax Independent Company, "and equals we shall go out of it. All men are by nature born equally and free."

He was ashamed that Virginia was the first English colony in America to have slaves.

The first Negroes in Virginia were indentured servants, who could earn their freedom. But within fifty years the status of the black man was changed. Slavery was recognized in the law of the colony.

Slaves were in all the colonies, north and south. But in the years immediately preceding the Revolution, colony after colony expressed displeasure over importation of slaves from abroad. There was a fear of slave uprising, but, also, feeling grew that slavery was wrong. The Quakers taught that it was against the word of God and prepared the Negroes for freedom by teaching them to read and write. Colonies began to pass laws forbidding the importation of any more slaves. In 1774, Virginia, where human freedom was held dear, voted to end the foreign slave trade.

When the American Revolution began, many slaves and free Negroes offered to bear arms against the British. The slaves wanted to be free and hoped all the new talk of liberty would include them. Except for New England, the state that recruited the largest number of Negroes into the fighting forces was Virginia. It enlisted over five hundred Negro soldiers and sailors.

In the army, some were drummers, marching into battle side by side with their white comrades. In the Continental Navy, the Negroes generally served in low ranks, such as powder boy and officer's boy, but on the waters of Chesapeake Bay they were often used as pilots.

They saw plenty of action on the Bay. One slave pilot named "Minny" lost his life when he was trying to board an enemy supply ship that was raiding the Rappahannock. Another, named Caesar, the slave of Carter Tarrant of Hampton, steered the schooner *Patriot* in many engagements and became famous. He was at the wheel when the *Patriot* captured a brig carrying stores for the British troops.

The Negroes also became guides, messengers and spies for the troops

Portsmouth today

of the new nation. Slave James, of New Kent County, outside Williamsburg, crossed Chesapeake Bay to Benedict Arnold's base at Portsmouth. Under secret orders, he furnished information during the critical spring of 1781 and won high praise from General Lafayette.

The British were active in using the Negro slaves, too. They wanted to deprive the Americans of the Negro muscle that forged munitions, drove wagons and built fortifications. They would seize and carry off slaves whenever possible.

The British also used the lure of freedom. Slaves escaped on foot and through the waterways. Chesapeake Bay tributaries were especially inviting and Virginia's Navy Board ordered the state galleys to cruise the rivers in order to prevent the flight of slaves.

The slaves escaped by the tens of thousands, despite all efforts to control them. Often they offered to serve in the British army and aboard royal vessels. Almost 15,000 sailed away with the British at the end of the war.

It would be a long time before the dark-skinned Virginians would feel they shared in the legacy of George Mason, or before the light-skinned Virginians would fully understand that the master of Gunston Hall had bequeathed to his state more than a plantation house.

65

Chapter 9

An Old Place on the Potomac

Several times each year my two youngsters and I enjoy visiting a special old farm. The drive takes only ten minutes on the parkway along the Potomac River. We have come to love this trip, as we love Virginia.

Many new homes have been built on the bluff above the road, but still we pass fragments of woods and marshes, and sometimes see ducks swimming, birds flying, a rabbit scampering for cover and a fearful turtle crawling as fast as he can out of the road. April and May are the liveliest time of year, when the trees and shrubs of Virginia are in bloom — the soft white and pink dogwood, redbud, wild azalea, crab apple and forsythia. In all seasons there is the Potomac, the river that has been more involved in American history than any other river, and that flows past Washington, our capital city fifteen miles north of us.

It is a wide and wonderful river of many moods, sometimes icy, sometimes choppy with high waves, sometimes smooth as glass and

Mt. Vernon

flecked with ships and small boats. The Indians knew it as the river of "traveling traders," the Patawomeke. From the early days when it offered the English settlers a profitable fur trade, it has helped to make America rich.

When we reach the old farm, we like to walk and see the two oldest and tallest trees on the grounds. You can learn a lot by knowing a tree — about the farmer who planted it and the kind of place he kept, perhaps even about the people of his time.

These two trees are called tulip poplars, even though they have no relation to either a tulip or a poplar but actually belong to the magnolia family. They are giants, nearly one hundred twenty feet tall, with straight trunks, deeply furrowed. Looking up we can see their glossy, long-stemmed leaves trembling in the slightest breeze. Their tulip-like blossoms, a blend of greenish yellow tinged with orange, are a welcome source of nectar to honeybees in early spring.

Hardly any American tree has a richer tradition than the tulip poplar. The Indians and early settlers hollowed dugouts of it. It was called the "canoe tree." "Everyone," wrote William Byrd II in his early colonial book, *Natural History of Virginia*, "has some of these trees in his gardens and around the house, for ornament and pleasure." As for the farmer who planted these two trees over one hundred and sixty-five years ago, certainly he would be proud of them today, towering, vigorous and still growing. For he was a man who loved the land and was endowed with faith in its future.

Our neighbor down the Potomac, of course, was George Washington, and his farm is Mount Vernon.

He chose to dwell at Mount Vernon although he had seen and known as much of Virginia as any man of his day. As a surveyor, soldier and land investor, he traveled from one end of the state to the other, from the Great Dismal Swamp to the high Appalachians. He experienced the hard ways of the wilderness and the gracious life of plantation mansions. These were his training grounds for leadership of a new nation.

What sort of person was Washington? He was shy and modest. He made no pretense at being witty and was not extremely talkative. He learned from experience and by listening to people around him. He was the kind of man who could dance gaily at a Palace ball in Williamsburg even after the royal governor dissolved the House of Burgesses and tried to enforce the hated British laws. In the same week he would be among those present at a secret meeting of the Virginia Assembly.

Visitors called frequently at his home on the Potomac. He regarded Mount Vernon as "a well resorted tavern, as scarcely any strangers, who are going from north to south, or from south to north, do not spend a day or two at it." But his main interest and activity were directed to his farming and gardening. His estate was made up of eight thousand acres. More than half of it was in woodland, and the remainder divided into five separate farms tilled by several hundred farmhands. Their little cabins dotted the estate. Each farm was devoted to special crops, the principal ones being wheat, Indian corn and tobacco. His ambition was not simply profit. He wanted to be the "first farmer of the country" and was delighted when he was awarded a silver cup for raising a prize jackass. He practiced crop rotation, planted in such a way as to stop erosion, and fertilized — at a time when most Potomac planters were destroying the fertility of their land by concentrating on tobacco only.

All that remains today is the homestead, or "mansion-house farm," but when my children and I visit Mount Vernon we walk down to the old river landing, where vessels embarked for England laden with great quantities of tobacco and flour ground in the Mount Vernon mill, each barrel bearing the widely known brand, "George Washington, Mount Vernon."

The town George Washington frequented was Alexandria, where he had been an apprentice surveyor and laid out the city lots. It was a thriving seaport, a rival of Baltimore or Boston in those days, with warehouses filled with goods, and the cobbled streets lined with fine town houses built by Scottish merchants. It was also on the stagecoach route, called the King's Highway, between Williamsburg and New England.

There were horse races, theater, ship launchings and cock fights. Card playing, drinking and gambling were enjoyed generally, and the best taverns, like the Indian Queen and Bunch of Grapes, had billiard tables. One of Washington's favorites was Gadsby's, a famous inn on Royal Street. He had his headquarters at Gadsby's when he was a colonel in the Virginia militia. Later he would attend his last birthday celebration before his death at this tavern. "Fall out, men, the wars are over," he said then after reviewing his beloved Alexandria troops.

Washington, a member of Masonic Lodge Number Twenty-two, became the grand master after the Revolution. When Christ Church was opened, he purchased pew number sixty for thirty-six pounds and ten shillings. This beautiful church, like much of "Old Town" in Alexandria, is still in use today. Washington's pew is marked with his name. So is the pew of Robert E. Lee, the son of his close friend.

Mainly, Washington attended services at Pohick Church, south of his house in the country, until it fell into disuse after the Revolution. He, George Mason and George William Fairfax all served on the building committee under which the church was constructed in 1769. He and his close friend, George Mason, of Gunston Hall, disagreed on the best location for the church. Washington, the trained surveyor, studied the entire parish. He drew a map showing roads, houses and distances, and then claimed he had located the point nearest to most members!

During the two years and nine months between his retirement in

Woodlawn

1797 and his death, Washington never went more than twenty miles from his home in northern Virginia. Most of the time he was the old farmer, content with improving his property. Occasionally the cream-colored coach he had used as President would be brought out, six blooded horses attached, and with servants in livery, away would go the former President and his wife. They would pay calls in the country or visit their friends in Alexandria. On other occasions, aboard a barge rowed by six servants, Washington would travel downriver to visit George Mason.

He devoted himself to his two adopted children, Eleanor, or Nelly, and George Washington Parke Custis. On his last birthday, February 22, 1799, Nelly was married at Mount Vernon to Captain Lawrence Lewis, the General's aide and nephew. As a wedding gift he presented them with two thousand acres of the Mount Vernon estate. He selected the site for their house on Gray's Hill. His friend, Dr. William Thornton, the first architect of the Capitol in Washington, agreed to design the new house, named Woodlawn.

Nelly's brother, George, built a different kind of house north along the Potomac, overlooking the capital city. It was constructed during the period of "Greek revival" architecture, when builders went back to the classical age for inspiration. Hardly any house has ever shown more grace or dignity than his home, Arlington, with its portico of stout white columns supporting a massive pediment, and balancing wings on either side.

As a boy growing up in Alexandria, Robert E. Lee often visited Arlington House. He played with Mary, the daughter of Mr. and Mrs.

Tomb of the Unknown Soldier, Arlington

Custis, who was about his own age, romping among the giant oaks, the groves of walnut, chestnut and elm. In 1831, one year after his graduation from West Point, he returned to marry Mary. After the death of Mr. Custis, Arlington became their home. And it was from Arlington that Lee departed to take command of the Confederate Army.

With the outbreak of the Civil War, the Arlington estate was fortified as part of the defense line around Washington. Overnight, the quiet country estate was transformed into a vast military encampment. It was used as a field hospital after the first battle of Manassas. The first burials were made in May, 1864, and have continued to the present day. By 1965, Arlington National Cemetery had become the resting place of nearly 130,000 servicemen and women, their wives, husbands and minor-age children. In this hallowed Virginia soil are the final remains of the Unknown Soldiers of World Wars I and II and the Korean War. Here lie two Presidents, William Howard Taft and John F. Kennedy.

Today Arlington is considered almost a part of the city of Washington. Alexandria, and Mount Vernon, are regarded as suburbs. This may be, but the soil remains Virginia's. The beauty of these places is that they live on and endure.

In Fredericksburg and Alexandria there are many clapboard and brick houses two hundred years old. Obscure little alleys lead to converted stables, and iron gates in high brick walls open into gardens of flowers and shrubbery.

Fredericksburg was close to Washington's heart. As a boy at Ferry Farm, he lived two miles outside the city, where he was supposed to have cut down that little cherry tree and tossed the legendary, but unlikely, silver dollar across the river. He often visited members of his family here, including his mother, for whom he provided a neat frame house till she died. His sister, Betty Lewis, lived with her husband in the noted mansion, Kenmore. His brother, Charles, operated the Rising Sun Tavern, a gathering place for patriots before the Revolution.

Old Pohick Church is now on the side of a busy highway, but when you step inside it will look much the same as the "first farmer of the country" knew it. The congregation meets regularly and all visitors are welcome.

73

Chapter 10

Mr. Jefferson's Hard Road

Thomas Jefferson was a pioneer who blazed new trails of the mind and spirit that are the cornerstone of democracy.

"I have sworn upon the altar of God eternal," he said, "hostility against every form of tyranny over the mind of man."

His road was not easy. Probably no leader in all American history created more that is new, and in so many fields — from architecture to botany to statesmanship. But Thomas Jefferson was opposed by many. His enemies denounced him as a dreamer, a Godless person, an evil man. The world still has not caught up with all his ideas of freedom and equality.

Jefferson's gifts to his native state, which he loved dearly, are among the greatest monuments to him. He was born at Shadwell, in Albemarle County, in 1743, and grew up on the democratic-minded frontier, among the foothills that smile up at the Blue Ridge. This was the land he knew best and to which he would always return.

Jefferson lived at a time when the Tidewater aristocracy was begin-

Monticello

ning to fade. The emphasis on the single crop, tobacco, had created wealth and destroyed wealth. Now leadership was coming from other sections. The first governor of the state, Patrick Henry, born in Hanover County, was a poor man who had had to borrow law books to study for his bar examination.

In 1760, seventeen-year-old Jefferson entered the College of William and Mary. He studied under Professor Wythe, his "faithful and beloved mentor," and after graduation became a very prominent lawyer.

He was elected to the House of Burgesses in 1769. He allied himself at once with the group led by Patrick Henry, that challenged the Tidewater gentry. He did not hesitate to speak out, calling some of the old planter class "cyphers of aristocracy."

Jefferson married a young widow, Martha Skelton, who brought him considerable property. They settled in a one-room cottage at Monticello, the mountain estate overlooking Charlottesville, and he began to design a beautiful home. It would be thirty years before it was fully completed. Many of the materials were brought from England, Italy and France. Much more, however, came from his inventive mind — disappearing beds on pulleys, great arched alcoves, folding doors, a dumbwaiter, and a big clock that records hours and days, and rings bells on the roof. Today it still works.

This was his dream house, filled with gadgets. But the design itself was no gadget to him. He was striving to create an American form of architecture, a natural style free of the English box-like Georgian influence (named for the period of King George).

Jefferson did open a new age of American architecture and could have been famous for that pioneer contribution alone. Later he designed the State Capitol, like a classical temple of the New World. When a prize competition was announced for a design for the Capitol in Washington, Jefferson entered under an assumed name and he almost won.

Politics soon crowded his life. His talents were recognized and he rose to leadership in Virginia and in the newborn nation. The Declaration of Independence, which he drafted in Philadelphia in 1776, was far more than a document of defiance against a distant king. It was a hymn to freedom — a hymn that inspires each generation to new deeds and loftier dreams.

The Virginia of 1776 was still far from a true democracy. It was controlled by the slaveholders. Land was unevenly distributed. Most of it was owned by the wealthy few. The right to vote was limited. The Episcopal Church was the "established" church, favored by law. Only children of rich families could obtain an education.

When Jefferson became governor, his goal was to form a greater Virginia, where "every trace would be eradicated of ancient or future aristocracy, and a foundation laid for a government truly republican."

His first step was the abolition of the laws of primogeniture and entail. Under those old laws, land always passed to the eldest son of a family, and so large estates could never be broken up. Great opposition was mustered against him, but Jefferson pushed through his reform. Since the right to vote in this period was based on landholding, breaking up the estates meant increasing the number of voters. One step forward for democracy.

He sponsored a law that made it easier for thousands of Scotch-Irish and German immigrants in western Virginia to become citizens and to vote. That was another step forward.

Hard battles were waged in the legislature to secure freedom for all religious faiths — or, more correctly, for freedom of conscience — and to separate church and state. He had devoted support from his friend James Madison, who later followed him as President of the United States. Together they rejoiced at the passage of the mighty Virginia Statute of Religious Liberty in 1786.

One of Jefferson's most important bills called for a public school system, in which the most able students would be sent to a state university. But the wealthy objected to paying taxes to educate the poor and the bill was defeated. Education remained a luxury. A new generation of leaders was not trained. Virginia, as well as Jefferson, was the loser.

Jefferson failed also in his attack on slavery. The legislature voted that any slave brought into the state and kept there one year would become free. This discouraged importing slaves from Africa, but that was as far as it went.

But Jefferson was encouraged. He believed that Virginia had produced the first legislature with courage "to declare that the reason of man may be trusted with the formation of his own opinions."

Jefferson served as governor during one of the darkest periods of the Revolution. At the urgent request of General Washington, he had stripped Virginia of nearly all its troops in order to aid the Continental cause. When the state was invaded by the British in 1780, Governor Jefferson was widely blamed for the lack of effective defense. He and members of the Governor's Council were almost captured when they fled Richmond for refuge in Charlottesville.

They were saved through the alertness of a young innkeeper, Jack Jouett. He had left the Swan Tavern in Charlottesville to spend an evening at another inn, the Cuckoo Tavern. There he caught wind of the Redcoat plot. Colonel Banastre Tarleton and his men were headed straight for Charlottesville. Jack rode hard and fast through the night to warn Jefferson and the Assembly members. Jefferson was able to escape to a friend's home in Albemarle County. His capture would have been one of the worst disasters of the war.

One misfortune after another befell him. He was thrown from a horse and could barely get about. His beloved wife died in 1782. He decided to quit public life. Like Washington, he was never ambitious for personal power.

In the quiet of his home, Jefferson wrote a book called *Notes on the State of Virginia*, which became one of the finest, perhaps *the* finest, ever written about this state. For many years it was a popular handbook, with its descriptions of beautiful scenery, details of history and geography.

Meanwhile, his conduct as governor during the invasion was completely vindicated by the Assembly. He was not to remain a private citizen, but was chosen to go to Congress. He went on to fill one high position after another — Minister to France, Secretary of State under Washington, Vice-President and President of the United States. These were hard years in the early life of a young country. It was not always certain that democracy would thrive and grow. Jefferson played a large part in making sure that it did.

Jefferson became third President of the United States. He broadened national vistas by completing the famed Louisiana Purchase, paying Napoleon's government in France the small sum of $15,000,000 for its claims to the vast territory between the Mississippi River and the Rocky Mountains. He foresaw the great new western country as a place where struggling Americans could acquire their own small farms and share the fruits of the land.

He decided to send an expedition overland to explore the Rockies and continue to the Pacific Ocean. Such a hazardous journey into un-known territory had not been made before in the United States. For leaders of the expedition, he chose two Virginians, his own private secretary, Captain Meriwether Lewis, who had served with distinction in the old Northwest Territory, and William Clark, brother of the intrepid George Rogers Clark. With a party of thirty-two men, Lewis and Clark headed up the Missouri River from St. Louis on May 14, 1804. They blazed trails through thousands of miles of wilderness in the best tradition of earlier Virginia explorers like John Smith and George Washington. They would not return until September, 1806, but they brought back vast information about the mighty rivers, the climate, plants, animals and Indians.

Captain Lewis gave the greatest effort of his life to the Northwest. One year later while in St. Louis, as governor of the Louisiana Terri-tory, he was in financial difficulties and mentally upset. He decided to ride back to Washington to see the President. On the way he com-mitted suicide and was buried at the side of the Natchez Trace in Tennessee.

The death of Meriwether Lewis was a hard blow for Thomas Jeffer-son. But as with men of true greatness, he learned to endure the bitter. He had opponents in high places but he had close friends, like James Madison and James Monroe, whom he could rely on. Those three were almost like brothers. They shared common beliefs and fought side by side. They followed each other, one, two, three as President of the United States.

James Madison, of Orange County in the Piedmont region, was known as "little Jeemy," for his small stature. Everyone respected his brilliance and honesty. Throughout his life, he was the tireless cham-pion of freedom of religion and conscience. He earned the title of "Father of the Constitution," for planning the system of checks and balances among the legislative, executive and judicial branches of our government at the Constitutional Convention of 1787. When Jefferson was elected President, it was only natural that he should ask his first lieutenant, Madison, to be his Secretary of State.

This devotion continued to the end of their lives. Following his two terms as President, Madison helped Jefferson organize the University of Virginia. He loved the University and Jefferson so much that he be-

79

came Rector of the University after the death of Thomas Jefferson.

James Monroe followed Madison as President. Born on the Northern Neck, he fought in the Revolution as a young lieutenant-colonel. He studied law under Jefferson and opened his own practice in Fredericksburg. But he was drawn to politics and to Jefferson. In 1788 he moved to Charlottesville. Jefferson was pleased and chose the site of Monroe's home, Ash Lawn, on the crest of the very next hill.

When Monroe was asked by Madison to become Secretary of State, it meant his resignation as governor of Virginia, but he resigned. When the War of 1812 was going badly, he took on the added job of Secretary of War. This is probably the only time in history that one man has held both these Cabinet positions.

Monroe's eight years as President meant that Virginia's Three Musketeers occupied the White House for twenty-four consecutive years. He was the "last of the cocked hats" of the Revolutionary "Virginia dynasty" on the national scene. At the end of his term, Monroe retired to Oak Hill, his cream-colored brick mansion near Leesburg.

Jefferson had foes as brilliant as his friends. One was Alexander Hamilton, who served with him in Washington's Cabinet. They became chief spokesmen for two opposing points of view. Hamilton believed the young republic must have a strong central government. Jefferson felt that all people must determine the nation's destiny, living under as little government control as possible. They watched each other very carefully and President Washington watched them both. It is difficult to say that one was right and the other wrong, or how they might express themselves about circumstances today.

This would apply also to Jefferson's long controversy with John Marshall, his kinsman and fellow Virginian. Marshall was a cousin of Jefferson, but the two were never friendly. Born in a log cabin on the Piedmont frontier of Fauquier County, Marshall fought in several fierce battles of the Revolution. As he would say later, he had entered the army a Virginian and had come out an American — thus it became Marshall's belief that only through a strong central government could the United States be an effective nation.

John Marshall became the fourth Chief Justice of the United States.

Beginning in 1801, he served thirty-four years, longer than any other Chief Justice in history. He became the principal architect of the American system of constitutional law. It was Justice Marshall who established the power of the Court to declare laws unconstitutional and the doctrine that federal power must prevail over state power if the two did not agree. Through his firm statements the Supreme Court and the entire judicial system gained respect and dignity. So too did the Constitution as the basic charter of the land.

Jefferson fought issues, rather than individuals. Following his democratic principles, he sought again and again to abolish slavery and to keep it from spreading into the western territories. But he was blocked by the Deep South cotton planters and Northern slave traders. Finally he succeeded in obtaining a law prohibiting the importation of slaves, and he regarded this as one of his major achievements.

The University of Virginia

Mr. Jefferson was saddened by the failure to realize his cherished "empire of liberty." He yearned for home. Finally, at the age of sixty-five, he retired from the Presidency and the "hated occupation of politics" and turned toward Monticello.

But for him it was not the end. Now he concentrated on his long efforts to establish the University of Virginia, the "academical village" of his dreams. He set to work designing the entire campus, from the great circular rotunda to the colonnades of student quarters, professors' houses, the garden, and the winding serpentine wall. He supervised construction. Sometimes he watched the workmen with a spyglass from the mountainside at Monticello. When the university opened in 1825, Thomas Jefferson was the Rector, or president.

After all the years of public service, his wealth was gone. But wealth was never his goal. Nor could the wealthiest man in the world direct that the epitaph upon his gravestone be engraved, as did Jefferson, with such words as these:

Here Was Buried
THOMAS JEFFERSON
Author
of the Declaration of
American Independence,
of
the Statute of Virginia
for Religious Freedom, and
Father of the University
of Virginia

Chapter 11

Prelude to Civil War

There is an old plantation, formerly called the Burroughs place, near Smith Mountain Lake on the Roanoke River, in Franklin County. Its history reveals a vital chapter in the Virginia story. It was an ordinary farm, typical of the Piedmont and the mountains. The main crops were tobacco, corn, oats, wheat and flax. Instead of living in a lovely mansion surrounded by magnolia and legends, the master of the plantation lived in a plain cabin and worked in the fields from sunup to sundown alongside his slaves.

The Burroughs place shows how many Virginians lived, and what they dreamed. It helps explain why the war was fought that tore Virginia — and the nation — apart.

In a dirt-floored slave cabin a child was born five years before the Civil War erupted. He had no family name but he came to be known as Booker T. Washington. The old plantation where he was born is now a national monument commemorating his life and his rise from slavery to national renown.

The Piedmont region

Some people said the slaves were treated very well, that the Negro was better off in slavery. A prominent Virginia editor, George Fitzhugh, wrote long ago: "The children and the aged and infirm work not at all, and yet have all the comforts and necessaries of life provided for them. They enjoy liberty, because they are oppressed neither by care nor labor."

Booker T. Washington did not view it just this way, however, in his childhood slave cabin in Franklin County. Mr. Washington was a man who grew to be very influential and well respected by Presidents of the United States and white industrial leaders. But he never forgot his birthplace in slavery.

Booker's home was a tiny one-room log cabin with a dirt floor and a fireplace but no windows. In the center was the "potato hole," a large opening where sweet potatoes were kept for his master's family. Food for the slaves was a piece of bread or a scrap of meat, a cup of milk one time, some potatoes at another. After it was dark and still, in the late hours of the night, when the children had been without sufficient food during the day, his mother would rouse them. The youngsters would find she had got from somewhere eggs or parts of chicken and had cooked them during the night for the children.

When he was six, Booker was given a "tow shirt" to wear. A tow shirt looked like a short nightgown and was made of refuse flax, rough and coarse. Until it had been worn for about six weeks, it made one feel as if a thousand needle points were pricking his flesh. Soon after, Booker began to do light chores — taking corn to the mill, carrying water to men in the fields and shooing flies from his master's table.

Booker felt that Mr. James Burroughs, owner of the plantation, was above average in his treatment of slaves. Only a few times were they cruelly whipped. The deepest impression of slavery upon his mind came one morning when his uncle was stripped naked, tied to a tree, and whipped with a cowhide. As each blow touched his back the cry, "Pray, master! Pray, master!" came from his lips.

The treatment of slaves varied. That depended on the kind of man the master was. Some masters were kind; they would ignore slave laws they felt were unfair. Perhaps the slaves best off were those who lived in towns. They occasionally were permitted to go out and seek their own employment; the money they earned could be used to purchase their freedom. Some slaves were given their freedom because of faithful service, or because their masters no longer believed that slavery was right. The free Negro had to carry a certificate issued by the courts. He did not necessarily want to go North, for he knew that land was no Eden for the colored man.

On a large plantation, slaves who worked in the "big house" usually were more fortunate than the field hands. They had special privileges and were given decent clothes or special uniforms to wear. They ate well and slept in beds, not pallets on the floor. Often they were taught to read and write, and had the chance to travel. These slaves were the plantation cook, coachman, butler, housemaid — and of course the "mammy," the loved slave nurse who raised the master's children.

Ranking just below them were the skilled craftsmen — the blacksmith and brickmason, the carpenter and harness maker. Many mansions and town houses all over the South that are admired today for their fine woodwork, balconies and wrought-iron grills were fashioned by black artisans.

Sometimes slaves ran away. They knew if they were caught they would be carried back in chains or thrown into the slave jail in Richmond. But they tried nevertheless. A group of white people called abolitionists, because they wanted to abolish slavery, helped the slaves on their dash to freedom by setting up the Underground Railroad. This "railroad" was made up of stations a day's journey apart. The escaping slaves were hidden in a barn or hayrack, and given food.

Slaves attempted uprisings, even though they could not succeed. The rebellion which had the greatest drama and disaster was led by Nat Turner, a slave preacher in Southampton County, of Southside Virginia. A deeply religious man, he believed that he had orders from God to free his people. Other slaves called him the "Prophet." On the night of August 21, 1831, he led a small band armed with crude weapons, knives, axes and sickles. The first to die were Nat's master and his family. Then the rebels headed down the road along the Nottaway River, gathering recruits among the blacks and inflicting death upon the whites. After forty-eight hours of nightmare, nearly sixty persons were dead. Nat Turner was not caught for six weeks. Then he was tried and hanged.

Nat Turner forced Virginia to face the slavery question. Within two months after his rebellion the General Assembly debated the issue with strong feelings and emotions.

It should be remembered that antislavery sentiment was almost as deep-rooted in Virginia as the institution of slavery itself. The mountain districts of western Virginia were vigorous in their opposition to slavery. So were Thomas Jefferson Randolph, grandson of Thomas Jefferson, and Thomas Marshall, son of the great Chief Justice, who led the fight in the Assembly to abolish slavery. But they lost. The vote was close, sixty-five to fifty-eight.

Slavery became a heated national issue, too. But it was cotton, not tobacco, that called the tune. There seemed to be no end to the demand. Vast fortunes were made out of endless bales of cotton, harvested by thousands of slaves in the Southern sun.

The sectional arguments grew hotter with the swiftly passing years. Slavery became the symbol of right and wrong, good and evil.

Virginia remained Union-minded, in contrast to the strong and violent feeling of the cotton states. Of course there were several Virginias — the Virginia of the large planters, and the small planters, the poorer whites in the Tidewater and Piedmont, the mountain people in the Blue Ridge and beyond, and the Negroes. Many views were expressed.

The state faced a problem of its own with the region west of the Blue Ridge. Those western counties complained they were being denied their rightful voice at the capital in Richmond. Planters of the Piedmont and Tidewater had much greater strength because their slaves counted in determining the number of representatives in the Assembly. The slaves did not vote and the planters paid no taxes on them. Yet these planters controlled the money to be spent on road improvements and canals. What was worse, they still wouldn't allow a free system of schools for all boys and girls.

In the beautiful mountains of western Virginia, the stormy 1850's felt their final thunderbolt. It was the raid of the fiery abolitionist, John Brown, and his band of men who hoped to arm the slaves and establish a free state in the hills.

Brown considered himself an instrument of Providence and became known as "God's angry man." His scheme was wild and it was doomed, though he goaded both sides to the brink of war from which there was no retreat. He made Harpers Ferry a name that would never be forgotten.

John Brown and his eighteen followers were drawn to Harpers Ferry because it was the site of a great rifle works (producing a thousand rifles and muskets a month) and a federal arsenal. On the night of October 16, 1859, they struck from the Maryland side of the Potomac. They captured the arsenal and held several hostages, but stirred little support for their insurrection. Shooting broke out with local residents.

The next night ninety marines arrived from Washington under command of Colonel Robert E. Lee and Lieutenant J. E. B. Stuart. God's angry man surrendered only after the marines stormed his brick "fort." In a swift trial at nearby Charles Town, he was convicted of treason against Virginia and of murder, and sentenced to be hanged. Riding on his coffin to the gallows, Brown spoke his last words; "This is a beautiful country." With that much of what he said, no one would disagree.

Harpers Ferry and Booker T. Washington's birthplace today are both national monuments. Both are part of the prelude to the drama of the Civil War that engulfed Virginia.

Chapter 12

Crucible of Fire

Traces of the Civil War are found scattered almost everywhere in Virginia. This was the main battlefield for the brave armies of both sides.

Battles of the war were fought in many parts of the United States, but fighting raged almost continuously across Virginia. The state teemed with marching men. It became the crucible of fire, the birthplace of heroism and self-sacrifice. It was the deathplace of thousands of good men, and the scene of destruction of livestock, cities, towns, railroads and bridges. These are the awful and unwanted prizes of war.

The war was fierce and cruel. The troops fought bitterly, as bitterly as enemies ever fought in warfare. But they held each other in high respect. Along the fighting front rarely did men hate.

It is known that sentries of Union and Confederacy would trade friendly insults, jokes, songs and smokes. After a bloody battle, the medical officers of one side would help treat the wounded of the other side. In the battle of Fredericksburg, in 1862, the Johnny Rebs were astounded by the courage of the Union troops charging up the steep

*Defense of Marye's Heights,
Fredericksburg*

slopes of Marye's Heights into withering point-blank fire. The Rebs cheered their foes.

Not every soldier was a hero. There were cowards, traitors and selfish men on both sides. But the pride, selflessness and valor of many soldiers and officers were unbounded. These were the men who could look their enemies squarely in the eye and salute them.

The federal army had great and undisguised admiration for Stonewall Jackson and for Jeb Stuart's artilleryman, John Pelham. No two men could have respected each other more than Grant and Lee when they finally met face to face at Appomattox to agree on terms of surrender. A few days later when President Lincoln visited Richmond, which had finally been taken after many attempts, he went to the home of General George Pickett, a hero of the Confederate cause. "Just say an old friend called," the President announced softly.

On one occasion General Robert E. Lee passed a wounded Union soldier on a field of battle. The trooper, spotting the military commander of the South, raised himself from the ground and shouted in defiance, "Hurrah for the Union!" The General stopped his horse, dismounted and came toward the man. The soldier in blue at first

90

thought that Lee meant to kill him. "But as he came up he looked down at me with such a sad expression upon his face that all fear left me," wrote the soldier later, "and I wondered what he was about."

General Lee extended his hand in friendship. He grasped the soldier's hand firmly and looked right into his eyes. "My son," he said, "I hope you will soon be well." That soldier kept himself erect and smiled in embarrassment and appreciation. But as soon as General Lee departed, he cried himself to sleep on the bloody ground.

These are the kind of stories the Civil War battlefields tell, stories that have inspired all generations since, and no doubt will inspire all generations to come.

Virginia had tried to avoid war. Even after the election of Abraham Lincoln, it had clung to its loyalty to the Union. It was South Carolina that led the split, declaring her secession from the Union in December, 1860. Within six weeks Mississippi, Florida, Alabama, Georgia, Louisiana and Texas followed. But there was much opposition even within some of those states.

Still Virginia refused to secede. It sought peace between North and South. Edmund Ruffin, a proud Virginia firebrand, was disgusted when the vote at the Capitol in Richmond went against secession by two to one on April 4, 1861. He decided to take his stand in South Carolina. Eight days after that vote was taken, Ruffin was among those who fired the first shots on Fort Sumter in Charleston Harbor.

Lincoln answered the Sumter fray at once by calling for 75,000 volunteers. In the emotional upsurge that followed, the moderate men who had led Virginia, North Carolina, Tennessee and Arkansas were swept aside. Those states now joined the Confederacy. Since Virginia had been undecided about which side to join, its decision boosted morale throughout the South. Richmond became the capital of the Confederacy.

In the mountain counties, the region that was later to be West Virginia broke away from the Old Dominion. Most people there were loyal to the Union. Their new government was known as the Restored State of Virginia until the new state of West Virginia was established.

Families and friends were as divided in their beliefs as the mountains were from the Piedmont and Tidewater. Thomas J. Jackson of West Virginia became a military hero of the Confederacy. His own sister, Laura Jackson Arnold, gave her loyalty to the Union. Some of Virginia's bravest sons were officers of the United States Army. General George H. Thomas, of Rockingham County, became known as the "Rock of Chickamauga" for his bravery, but his kinsmen at home turned his portrait to the wall.

Robert E. Lee felt the inner torment between his heart and his head, between support of his own state and the Union. He opposed slavery as an evil. He felt in his bones that secession was wrong. But when Lincoln offered him command of the Union Army at the outbreak of war, Lee followed the dictates of his heart. He placed himself as a Virginian first, an American second.

Did he choose the right course? No man can dictate the conscience of another. Robert E. Lee, like George Washington, has been transformed by many writers from human form into godly form. He was not perfect; he had flaws. His generalship on the field of battle has been criticized by many military experts. But Robert E. Lee did what he felt his duty demanded. No man could be called upon for more. He is remembered as a great Virginian and a great American. For four years he stood off superior numbers on the battlefields.

The opening battle was fought on a pleasant summer day at Manassas. The Yankees called it Bull Run. Before the day was done the Confederates had snatched a victory. And the strange bearded man in butternut and gray, named Thomas J. Jackson, had a new nickname. "Look!" shouted another officer. "There stands Jackson like a stone wall! Rally behind the Virginians!" He became known as Stonewall Jackson.

But the Yankees kept coming. Richmond was their target. They tried every way they knew to invade and capture it.

During 1862, the Union armies landed on the Virginia Peninsula. They occupied old Yorktown and headed toward Richmond. They came down through the Shenandoah Valley. They crossed the Rappahannock in boats and captured Fredericksburg, halfway from Washington to the Confederate capital. At Marye's Heights in Fredericksburg, you can see where Longstreet's Confederate troops, four deep, fired point blank at charging waves of Union soldiers.

The next year the armies met in the wooded fields at Chancellorsville. Lee turned back the Union soldiers, but lost Stonewall Jackson. He was killed by a stray bullet fired by one of his own men. Jackson was one of the fantastic men of the Civil War, a homely man who had been an ordinary instructor at the Virginia Military Institute. But on the battlefield "Old Jack" and his horse "Little Sorrel" moved like one, here, there, everywhere, always inspiring his troops.

There were many men of this breed. They fought for Virginia, they fought for their pride in the state. The planter class sent some of its finest men in their wide-brimmed sombreros and riding boots. They were men of a gallant age. The humble class sent some of its finest, too, singing the songs of "Ole Virginny," sometimes fighting like mobs, other times marching in tight ranks despite torn uniforms and bruised feet. Sometimes they had no shoes at all. Still they marched and fought, barefoot and bone-weary.

The final phase of the war began in 1864 when Ulysses S. Grant was placed in command of the Union army in Virginia. He, like Stonewall Jackson, showed talents for leadership and victory during wartime which were never evident in his civilian life.

Grant and Lee now squared off on Virginia soil. In the fierce Battle of the Wilderness, the woods caught fire, making an inferno in which

93

helpless wounded men died screaming in the flames. Grant pressed onward, from one side, then another.

The two main armies met at Spotsylvania, then again at Cold Harbor, one of the most harrowing battles of the war. Grant was forced to swing south, crossing the James River on a large pontoon bridge, to Petersburg. He began ten months of deadly siege that cut the supply lines into Richmond and starved the city.

Large portions of the state were devastated during the war, by fighting or by deliberate destruction. Lovely Shenandoah Valley was a particular target of federal troops under Phil Sheridan because it was a prime source of food supplies for the South. Many houses were burned and crops ruined.

Finally the end came at Appomattox.

Starving and outnumbered, Lee's army had moved southwest, toward Danville, hoping to join with local forces in North Carolina. But Grant pressed the pursuit hard.

On Palm Sunday, April 9, 1865, Robert E. Lee stopped retreating. His first hope that morning was to attack, not to surrender. The Confederates succeeded at first in brushing aside a thin line of Union cavalry. Next they ran into strong formations of the blue-coated infantry that would not yield. It was the end. A message was sent to U. S. Grant asking for a meeting to arrange the surrender.

The village of Appomattox between Richmond and Lynchburg stands the way it did in April, 1865. Imagine you can see the principal figures and hear their voices.

U. S. Grant rides up to the village about 1:30 P.M. astride his large black horse "Cincinnati." He pauses to ask a group of Union officers already there if General Lee has arrived.

"Yes," replies one, "in that brick house." He points to a structure in a locust grove. The house belongs to a man named Wilmer McLean.

Grant climbs the steps, wearing the uniform of a common soldier. His boots and breeches are spattered with mud. The only way you can tell his rank is by the three stars on his shoulder straps. He wears no sword.

Lee rises from his chair in the parlor. The gray-bearded general is dressed immaculately. He is poised and outwardly calm, the imperishable picture of a gentleman and a soldier, though he is a tired and old man. They look squarely into each other's eyes for a wordless instant.

94

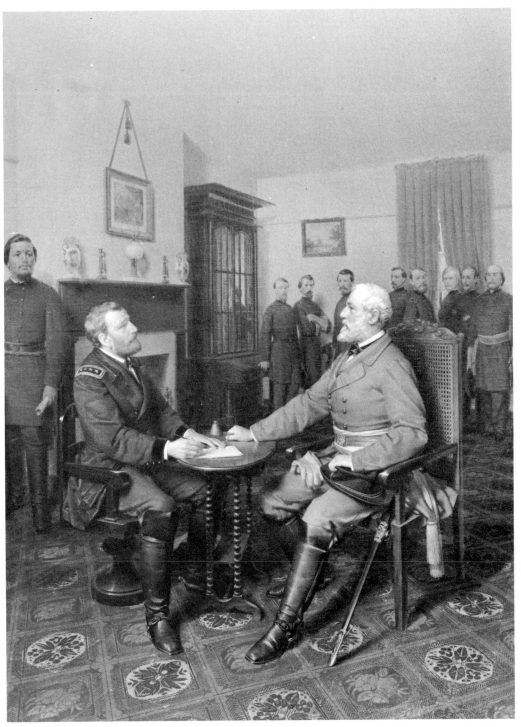

The surrender at Appomattox Court House

They talk for a few moments about the old army days and the Mexican War. Grant's officers remain at a respectful distance. Then the two turn to the business at hand. Grant demonstrates his generosity. The Confederates, who have been marching for days on empty stomachs, are to be furnished rations. Officers will keep their sidearms and horses. Men in the ranks who own horses or mules can keep them to work their little farms.

By four o'clock the business is done. Lee prepares to leave on the big iron-gray horse "Traveller." He raises his hat and rides out of the village, back across the Appomattox River to tell his men that he has surrendered the Army of Northern Virginia. "Men, we have fought the war together," he will say. "I have done my best for you; my heart is too full to say more."

Grant and his staff officers, standing silent and bare-headed, watch him ride off. They do not feel or act like conquerors. Soon, in the back of McLean's yard, Union soldiers will pick violets and daffodils to send to their sweethearts in the North, where the flowers bloom later than in Virginia. They hope to be home in time to see those blossoms in their own yards. There will be no more battles for them.

"Now, my children, we are free," said Booker T. Washington's mother. They had been called to the "big house" at the Burroughs farm, only sixty miles southwest of Appomattox. Excitement ran high as they heard the announcement that the war was over and that a new life was about to begin for them.

Emancipation would create problems. For many slaves it meant bewilderment and confusion. For Booker T. Washington it meant a challenge to earn a place of respect in the world. He worked at a salt furnace and in coal mines, teaching himself the alphabet. When he was sixteen he started to walk the five hundred miles for Hampton, to attend the Institute there, accepting rides when they were offered. He had the same inspiring will to win as other great sons of Virginia.

As Thomas Jefferson had created the University of Virginia, so did young Booker Washington, in his early twenties, establish a Negro normal school at Tuskegee, Alabama, in 1881, to help the cause of the freed Negro. He devoted his life to helping his people on the long, hard road from dependence in slavery to independence in freedom.

Chapter 13

Fields and Factories

Broadway, Virginia, like New York's great thoroughfare, is a crowded and often noisy place. The people may be few in numbers and soft-spoken, but this Broadway lies in the heart of Rockingham County, the turkey center, which produces vast quantities of the best, and most talkative, turkeys in America.

Broadway lies in a high, cool valley between the Massanutten Mountain and Little North Mountain — the beautiful green country of the George Washington National Forest, filled with little places of forgotten history. It is hard not to bring up Virginia's history. Instead of remaining with the present, the inclination is to look at the past. But that is the way of Virginia.

Broadway turkeys and chickens, however, make up a lively part of Virginia's varied agriculture. Industrial development in the state has lagged behind for many years, but recently it has begun to grow.

Whether factories are really better than farms I cannot say. They seem to be more necessary for prosperity in a modern age, although

97

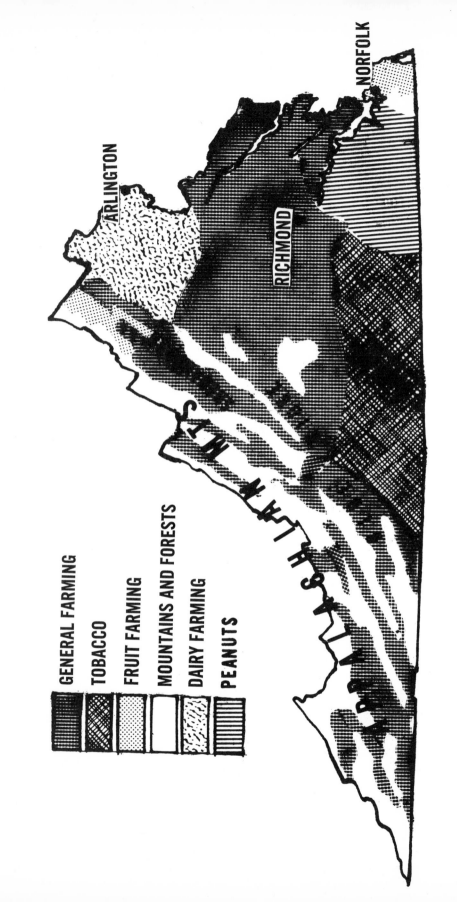

industry presents new problems. There is no better way of charting a healthy future than by helping young people to start thinking now about the changing shape of things.

The Virginia "money crop," for example, is tobacco. Danville, Petersburg, Lynchburg, South Hill and South Boston rank among the greatest tobacco markets of the United States. Danville alone can store 250 million pounds of tobacco in its warehouses. Farmers grow most of the tobacco south of the James River, in the "Southside" of the Piedmont. When you drive through southwestern counties you see fields covered with the golden-colored, thin-leaved burley. At Abingdon, the principal burley market, you can hear the chant of the tobacco auctioneer during winter sales. In Richmond, you cannot avoid the aroma of tobacco from warehouses and factories. You are welcome to visit several of the factories which produce over one hundred billion cigarettes a year, in addition to snuff, pipe tobacco, chewing tobacco and cigars.

Yet tobacco may be doomed. Cigarettes are harmful to the human body. This fact is established and accepted. Doctors all over America are now stressing this. In due course the popularity of tobacco will decline. What then of Virginia?

In Virginia, corn grows on more than six times as much land as tobacco. Farmers use corn and hay, another leading crop, chiefly to feed their livestock. Happily, several crops of hay can be harvested in one year, because of the mild climate, good soil and long growing season.

Besides the turkeys of Rockingham County, Virginia is a national leader in other items. Oysters and crabs are plentiful and Virginia is among the major menhaden-producing states. The processing industry is centered at Kilmarnock, on the Northern Neck.

South from there, across the Rappahannock, little Gloucester produces a commercial crop of real beauty — daffodils, in three hundred varieties, which brighten thousands of acres when they bloom in early spring. And south again, across the James River, Suffolk has the nickname "Peanut Capital of the World." In this region, peanut soup and peanut pie are table favorites. The section around nearby Smithfield is the home of the Smithfield ham, produced from hogs that roam through woods and fields during spring and summer and then are fattened on peanuts in the fall. After the killing, they are smoked slowly over smoldering hickory fires "to a rich mahogany hue" and stored for about a year.

On the Eastern Shore, farmers raise bumper crops of vegetables and sweet-tasting strawberries. Across the state, you can drive through miles of apple orchards, whose springtime beauty is celebrated in the Shenandoah Apple Blossom Festival held each year at Winchester. That city is said to have the world's largest apple storehouse and the world's largest plant for manufacturing apple products. Shenandoah Valley, the old "bread basket of the Confederacy," produces milk, hogs, beef cattle, poultry and winter wheat. Thoroughbred horse-and-cattle country lies east of the Valley, near Leesburg, Warrenton and Middleburg. Horses for fox hunting and racing are still raised on large estates in this section of the Piedmont.

As for manufacturing industries, shipbuilding yards at Norfolk and Newport News have for many years built all kinds of vessels, including giant aircraft carriers and passenger liners. Chemicals and chemical products are another important industry. Giant fertilizer plants line the rivers on the south shore of Hampton Roads. The Dan River Mills at Danville are considered the largest single textile plant in the world, using ninety million pounds of cotton a year. They make everything from sheets to beautiful dress materials.

In the southwestern mountains, the region beyond Roanoke called the Appalachian Plateau, coal is king. It is the most important mineral resource of the state and large quantities are concentrated in the fields of Tazewell, Dickinson, Buchanan and Wise Counties, the old rugged corner of frontier feudin' where Kentucky, West Virginia and Virginia meet. The famous Pocahontas beds have mined and shipped almost one and a half billion tons since the 1880's.

But King Coal sits uneasily on the throne. Poor mining practices have caused damage to the land. Seepage of acid drainage has killed fish in the streams. Lack of demand, low market prices and the introduction of mechanical equipment have brought lower employment in the hills. A beautiful section, the mining country; but its future may be more in its scenery, through the tourist industry, than its coal.

Among other minerals, clay, limestone, sand and gravel, manganese, mica, lead and zinc are yielded by the good Virginia earth. The state

Coal country

is the country's largest producer of soapstone, and of titanium, the strong, light metal used in aircraft jet engines.

Trees are part of the rich resource of Virginia. Years ago the trees in these forests were destroyed and despoiled. Millions of them were cut without any thought to the future of the priceless forests. It is difficult to find what is called a "virgin stand" or "first growth." But trees have grown again under careful management by the state, the federal government and large timber companies. Trees — for beauty and use.

Chapter 14

Long Valley, High Horizons

The longest distance between two points in Virginia is four hundred and seventy miles, as the crow flies, from Assateague Island, bathed by the waters of the Atlantic, diagonally across the state to Cumberland Gap, where Dan'l Boone blazed the famous Wilderness Road through the mountains.

In some ways, these two points are worlds apart.

The lay of the land that makes up each region is entirely different. One is composed of sand, swamp and marsh, the other of sheer cliffs 1,700 feet high, with panoramic views of deep green valleys.

You may not believe this, until you look at a map, but Cumberland Gap is twenty-five miles farther west than Detroit, Michigan. Yet it is still in the same Virginia that borders the Atlantic at sea level.

Traveling across Virginia, watch the landscape change. Trees and plants change as the rocks and soils change.

Beyond the light, sandy loam of the Tidewater, the gently rolling hills of the Piedmont are composed of thinner clay soils, with hard ground and rock near the surface. Then the great mountain wall

White Cliffs of the Cumberland Mountains

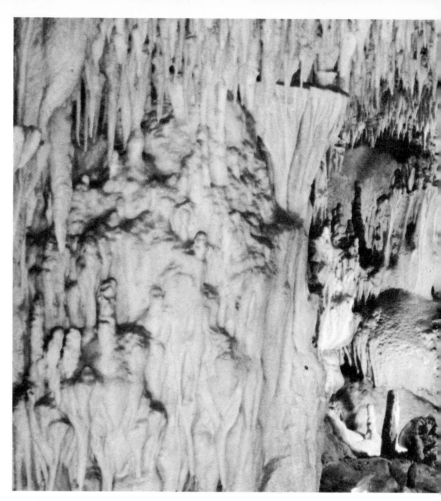

Massanutten Caverns

called the *Blue Ridge* rises abruptly along the western edge of the Piedmont. It is the eastern rampart of the Appalachian Mountains, the oldest mountain system on North America, formed out of the earth's crust millions and millions of years before the Rockies, Sierras or Cascades of the West.

West of the Blue Ridge lies the *Great Appalachian Valley*, composed of rich limestone soil. In different states it has different names. Here it is known as the Valley of Virginia, divided by ridges into six separate valleys. The largest of them is the beautiful Shenandoah. Beyond the Great Valley, the *Alleghenies* swing southwestward in wide ridges, reaching their greatest heights, up to 4,500 feet, along the line between Virginia, West Virginia and Kentucky.

The Great Valley, running from Winchester down to Bristol, be-

tween the Blue Ridge and the Alleghenies, has a special personality and importance of its own in the makeup of Virginia.

In colonial days the Valley provided the pattern of migration and settlement. The grandparents of Abraham Lincoln came down this way from Berks County, Pennsylvania, a little before their old neighbors, the Boones, with their young son, Dan'l, headed for the frontier in North Carolina. To them and thousands of others, the Valley was either a place to stop and build a home or to rest with old friends.

They found unusual natural wonders that still astound visitors. Among these are limestone caverns formed millions of years ago by the flow of ancient underground rivers, coupled with the constant seeping of acid-bearing water. As a result, layers of clay were washed away, leaving only great rooms and avenues of limestone decorated with stalagmite and stalactite formations. Of several caves open to the public, the Caverns of Luray are the best known. They compare with the most beautiful in the country. Far below the surface an ingenious organ has been installed producing music from the stalactites themselves through electronically controlled hammers.

Then there is the Natural Bridge, a towering limestone arch that Thomas Jefferson once owned. He described the great bridge, carved by Cedar Creek, as "the most sublime of Nature's works."

But Jefferson would be disappointed in it today. He resisted suggestions for man-made changes and said the bridge should always remain as Nature left it. Instead, it now supports the main road down the Shenandoah Valley. The view is blocked by a wooden fence, and Mr. Jefferson would have to pay a fee before gaining admission.

Natural Bridge

Cyrus Hall McCormick's farm

Staunton, on the other hand, is surrounded by fertile fields, blue-grass grazing lands and orchards. Here is the birthplace of one of the country's greatest Presidents, Woodrow Wilson. His father was a Presbyterian minister, and the manse where Woodrow was born has been restored as a shrine housing many of his personal possessions. He was somewhat like Jefferson, a learned man with deep faith in the people. The manse at Staunton is an excellent place for an introduction to Wilson and his beliefs.

South near Steele's Tavern is a shrine to a man who revolutionized farming — Cyrus Hall McCormick, the inventor of the mechanical grain reaper. He spent days, weeks and months tinkering about the crude blacksmith's shop that still stands. Most of the old farm is now managed by Virginia Polytechnic Institute for experimental purposes, a fitting memorial to the inventor. The gristmill and blacksmith shop, housing historic displays, are open to the public.

Lexington stands out as one of the most interesting and useful cities in all Virginia. It is the location of two fine colleges, both distinguished for their traditions and high standards.

One is the Virginia Military Institute, the "West Point of the South." Its graduates have taken a prominent part in every war since the Mexican War of 1846. Their most spectacular and heroic engagement occurred in the Valley when the entire corps of cadets was rushed into action against the Yankee tide at New Market in 1864. Stonewall Jackson was teaching at V.M.I. when the Civil War broke out. His body was brought back to Lexington for burial. Another Confederate hero, Commodore Matthew Fontaine Maury, "Pathfinder of the Seas," taught at V.M.I. after the war. And of many graduates who worked their way up from lowly "brother rats" to high command, the most illustrious was General George C. Marshall, chief of staff during World War II. He commanded an army of more than ten million Americans in all parts of the world. Although offered one million dollars for his memoirs, he presented them before his death to V.M.I., where they are housed in the impressive Marshall Research Library.

Robert E. Lee came to Lexington, too. He was wearing a gray uniform from which all the Confederate buttons had been removed. He became president of an old, run-down school called Washington College. "With the pen, in the five years before his death, he won a type of victory he had never been able to win with the gun." So wrote Professor Marshall W. Fishwick, while on the staff of Washington and Lee University, the school that the old general revived and shaped into an outstanding academic institution.

South of Roanoke, little Abingdon has achieved a measure of international renown as headquarters of the Barter Theatre. Begun by Robert Porterfield in the Depression years of the 1930's, it earned its name when all kinds of foods, from hams to huckleberries, were bartered for admission tickets. The theater furnished employment and inspiration to many actors who have gone on to star in New York and Hollywood. It continues to perform this role under Mr. Porterfield's guiding hand, though now it's strictly cash at the box office!

At Bristol, Virginia reaches its border, but not the long valley. Here you can stand on State Street with one foot in Virginia, the other in Tennessee. The Bristols are called "twin cities," but they are really one.

If you stay on the Virginia side, turn west and you reach the Cumberlands. Anyone who has read *The Trail of the Lonesome Pine* or *The*

Looking west from the Blue Ridge Parkway

Little Shepherd of Kingdom Come will want to visit Big Stone Gap, for it was here that John Fox, Jr., the author, found his inspiration for these and other stories of mountain people.

The Virginia mountains have a wonderful variety of trees, plants and animals. The best of our wooded wonders are protected for us, and in a way by us. They are within the national forests and national parks, the common property of all Americans. Some fine areas are in our state parks, too.

One of the nicest places I know to get the feeling of the Virginia mountain forest is at Elizabeth Furnace. Check the location on a map: the Furnace is in Fort Valley near the north end of Massanutten Mountain, the great ridge running through Shenandoah Valley for a distance of fifty miles.

Today, Elizabeth Furnace is an outstanding place to observe wildflowers, shrubs, trees, birds and animals. The forest is made up mainly of *hardwood* trees, those that shed their leaves each year and color the mountains with all shades of red, orange and yellow in the fall. *Softwood* trees, the conifers, or evergreens, grow here, too. The U. S. Forest Service has marked a nature trail, starting from the attractive campground and picnic area.

Elizabeth Furnace lies within the mighty George Washington National Forest covering one million acres in the Blue Ridge and the Alleghenies along the western boundary of the state. In the southwest section, the Jefferson National Forest consists of approximately 543,-000 acres. The dividing line between them is the James River. These two national forests play a vital role in the life of Virginia. They were created after 1912, when the federal government began buying lands in the mountains. The best trees had been cut by large logging companies who left nothing to grow in their place. Many forest fires and floods from the high mountains had run rampant. Farmers had given up the struggle to tame the stony soils and steep pastures.

Now, under the protection of forest rangers, trees are carefully logged for the lumber, furniture and pulp industries of the state. New trees reproduce themselves naturally from seeds, or are planted to insure continual growth, which foresters call *sustained yield*. The lands are safeguarded from fire and from flood. They furnish clean, clear water from the high mountain streams to many communities.

Most of the forest lands are open to hunting and fishing. They must be managed with care to make certain there will always be fish and animals in our woods. In cooperation with the Virginia Commission of Game and Inland Fisheries, the Forest Service regulates hunting. It opens clearings and plants trees that will furnish nuts for large animals, and special grasses the birds like to eat.

Elizabeth Furnace is only one of many recreational areas where forest visitors can camp or picnic and follow nature trails. A few, like Sherando Lake, near Waynesboro, have swimming beaches — and lots of swimmers.

Others, like Mount Rogers, fifteen miles from Marion, are for the hiker who wants to discover and enjoy the natural pleasures of Virginia. Mount Rogers (5,719 feet) is Virginia's highest peak. You can hike a wonderful trail up to the summit with a Scout troop or your parents through stands of Fraser fir, or balsam. This evergreen tree is usually found in Canada, far to the north, but the cool climate high on Mount Rogers makes the fir and spruce just "a bit of Canada in southwestern Virginia."

Near Mt. Rogers in the Jefferson National Forest

Virginia has excellent hiking trails in these western mountains. The most famous is the Appalachian Trail, one of the great boulevards of America. It extends 2,100 miles from Maine to Georgia. It places you in the world of self-reliance and self-propulsion, and everyone ought to try a portion of it. Virginia has the longest section of any state — five hundred miles, winding through both national forests and Shenandoah National Park. A splendid system of closed shelters is kept up by the Appalachian Trail Club.

Near Roanoke, on the beautiful Blue Ridge Parkway, the twin Peaks of Otter, Sharptop (elevation 3,875 feet) and Flattop (elevation 4,001 feet) have drawn sightseers since Jefferson's day. In 1852, the people of this area, wishing to make a contribution to the Washington Monument, then under construction, sent a large fragment of rock from the Peaks to Washington, D.C. Today it rests in the west wall of the monument, at the twelfth stairway landing, bearing this inscription:

> From Otter's summit,
> Virginia's loftiest peak,
> To crown a monument
> To Virginia's noblest son.

The nature trail at the Peaks offers a rare treat — the chance to see elk, or at least their tracks. Elk once ranged through the mountains until they were killed off by reckless game hunters. In 1917, a small herd was brought to Virginia from the Rocky Mountains. Under protection, the herd has survived well and grown.

The Blue Ridge Parkway is one of the marvels of modern Virginia. The idea of the Parkway was born, it is said, on a pleasant summer day in August, 1933, when President Franklin Delano Roosevelt came to Shenandoah National Park on an inspection tour. Shenandoah, covering 105 miles of the Blue Ridge, was still new then, not yet opened to the public. The President was enchanted with the panoramic views from the Skyline Drive winding along the mountain crest. When it was suggested by Harry F. Byrd, who served Virginia as Senator for many years, that a road might be constructed to connect Shenandoah with the Great Smoky Mountain National Park 469 miles away, the President became thoughtful. Could it really be done? When his best advisers told him that it would be costly and take a long time, the President asked more questions. At last he reached his decision. The Parkway was worth the time and effort. It would be built to enrich the future of Virginia, North Carolina and all America.

Today the Parkway provides quiet, leisurely travel, free of trucks and signboards, through the forested mountains. It is not a road, but a *way of travel*. A way to learn the land, and to love it.

The roadside, bordered with rhododendron, azalea, white pine and other native plants, blooms like a flower garden in spring. In summer it is cool and green, and in autumn it takes on the many hues of changing colors. Views are enlivened by highland farms, whose split-rail fences, weathered cabins and gray barns symbolize the culture of the hills.

Along the way are campgrounds, picnic areas and recreation centers like the Peaks of Otter. Each one tells a different part of the mountain and mountaineer story. Humpback Rocks, near Waynesboro, shows a group of log buildings of the pioneer days when the rule was "make it yourself or do without." You can see where the early cabins had small peepholes and two doors, one on the front and one on the back side, as a protection against Indians. You can learn how mountain people made their own banjos, or "banjers," as well as fiddles and "gee-tars." At the James River Overlook, near Glasgow, you can watch one of America's most beautiful rivers flow far below you enroute to the sea. The exhibits explain the story of the James River-Kanawha Canal, which became the main artery of commerce between Richmond and the valleys of western Virginia until the railroads doomed it to failure. At Mabry Mill, far south in Virginia, you can see a genuine water-powered gristmill in operation, grinding cornmeal and buckwheat flour the oldtime way. It may look crude, but getting all those iron gears and shafts to work just right took sheer genius.

I love to walk up to the overlooks along the Blue Ridge Parkway, or the Skyline Drive in Shenandoah National Park, with my two children. No two views are ever the same. Even a single scene will change from one hour to the next.

We see the Piedmont foothills to the east. We see the Great Valley, the route of the pioneers, to the west, and beyond it the massive Alleghenies. We hear the birds in flight. I point out to my children the raven, the great black bird of wilderness that dwells on crags where the wind-twisted oak and pine barely survive.

I think of the Indians, the hunters and warriors, who began mankind's adventure in the hills. I tell my children of John Muir, the great naturalist, who said, "The mountains are fountains, not only of rivers and fertile soil, but of men. Therefore, we are all, in some sense, mountaineers, and going to the mountains is going home."

We look to the high horizon. As far as we can see it is still Virginia. The land and sky are filled with adventures and mysteries and hopes for tomorrow.

Sharptop Mountain

Virginia Profile

Old Dominion

GENERAL

Statehood   June 25, 1788; tenth state to join the Union
Area   40,815 square miles; thirty-sixth-ranking state
Population   3,966,949 (1960 census); fourteenth-ranking state
Capital   Richmond
Motto   *Sic Semper Tyrannis*
          Thus Always to Tyrants
Flower   Flowering dogwood
Bird   Cardinal
Tree   Flowering dogwood (unofficial)
Song   "Carry Me Back to Old Virginia"

PHYSICAL CHARACTERISTICS

Boundaries

North   West Virginia and Maryland
East   Maryland and the Atlantic Ocean
South   North Carolina and Tennessee
West   West Virginia and Kentucky

Greatest width   452 miles east to west
Greatest length   209 miles north to south
Highest point   5,729 feet, Mt. Rogers
Lowest point   Sea level

Climate

Hot summers and short winters with some snow. Moderate rainfall. Highest recorded temperature: 110°. Lowest recorded temperature: −29°.

Principal cities

Norfolk: 305,872

Richmond: 219,958

Portsmouth: 114,773

Newport News: 113,662

Roanoke: 97,110

Alexandria: 91,023

Lynchburg: 54,790

Danville: 46,577

Petersburg: 36,750

Charlottesville: 29,427

Principal mountains

Appalachian Ridge

Blue Ridge Mountains

Massanutten Ridge

Mt. Rogers: 5,729 feet

Whitetop Mountain: 5,520 feet

Principal rivers

Appomattox

Clinch

Dan

Holston

James

New River

Potomac

Powell

Rappahannock

Roanoke

Shenandoah

York

Principal lakes

Drummond

LEADING PRODUCTS

Manufacturing

Wood products (furniture, paper, lumber), chemicals, processed foods, textiles, clothing, cigarettes, machinery, ships

Agriculture

Tobacco, hay, corn, peanuts, soybeans, apples, potatoes, Smithfield hams; livestock, including dairy products and turkeys

Minerals

Coal, zinc, stone, cement, clay, petroleum, lead, natural gas

Fishing

Oysters

Tourism

Historic sites, battlefields, famous old churches, colonial homes
Skyline Drive along the top of the Blue Ridge Mountains
Large natural caves and caverns
One national park, two national forests
Three national historic parks, six state forests, nine state parks

GOVERNMENT

United States Congress

Senators: 2
Representatives: 10

State Legislature

Senators: 40
Delegates: 100

Counties in Virginia: 96

HISTORY

1607   Jamestown was established by the Virginia Company of London.

1609   Captain John Smith left Jamestown for England.

1612   John Rolfe introduced tobacco cultivation.

1614   Tobacco exportation was begun. John Rolfe married Pocahontas.

1619   The House of Burgesses, America's first representative legislature, met in Jamestown. The first Negroes were brought to Jamestown, probably as indentured servants, by Dutch traders. One hundred young women were brought to the colony as wives for the settlers.

1622   Four hundred settlers were killed in an Indian uprising.

1624   Virginia was made a royal colony.

1642   Sir William Berkeley was appointed governor and remained at the post for ten years.

1676   Nathaniel Bacon led a rebellion against the government. Bacon died of fever the same year.

1693   The College of William and Mary was founded.

1699   The capital moved from Jamestown to Williamsburg.

1716   Governor Alexander Spotswood began an expedition which crossed the Blue Ridge Mountains and opened the Valley of Virginia.

1763   A proclamation by George III of England — an attempt to establish troops in the colonies, control growth in the western areas and raise money through taxation — provoked hostility.

1769   Resolutions passed by the House of Burgesses.

1773   Virginia led in establishing a committee of correspondence with the other colonies.

1774   The first state convention met.

1775   Governor Dunmore seized the powder supply at Williamsburg and infuriated the colonists. George Washington was chosen by the Continental Congress to command the Continental Army.

1776   Virginia declared its independence and adopted its first constitution. The Bill of Rights drafted by George Mason was adopted. The Declaration of Independence was written by a Virginian, Thomas Jefferson.

1781 Lord Cornwallis surrendered at Yorktown in the last battle of the American Revolution.

1784 Virginia gave up its claims to western lands to the United States.

1788 On June 25, Virginia became the tenth state to join the Union.

1789 George Washington, a Virginian, was elected first President of the United States.

1792 Kentucky was formed from three of Virginia's western counties.

1801–25 Three Virginians served as President of the United States: Thomas Jefferson (1801–09), James Madison (1809–17), and James Monroe (1817–25).

1801–35 John Marshall of Virginia served as Chief Justice of the United States.

1819 The University of Virginia was chartered.

1825 The University of Virginia was opened.

1831 Nat Turner led an uprising among the slaves.

1841 William Henry Harrison, born in Virginia, became President. Harrison died a month later, and Vice-President John Tyler, also a Virginian, became President.

1849 Zachary Taylor, another Virginian, became President.

1859 John Brown's raid on Harpers Ferry.

1861–65 Virginia seceded from the Union and became the major battleground of the Civil War.

1863 West Virginia was formed from the northwestern part of Virginia.

1870 Virginia was readmitted to the Union.

1902 The present state constitution was adopted.

1912 Woodrow Wilson became the eighth Virginian to be elected President.

1927 Governor Harry F. Byrd sponsored a reorganization of the state government.

1940–45 During World War II new industry was opened in the state.

1959 The first public school integration in Virginia took place in Arlington County and Norfolk.

1864 The Chesapeake Bay Bridge-Tunnel connecting Norfolk and the Eastern Shore was opened.

GOVERNORS

Patrick Henry	1776–1779	William Smith	1846–1849
Thomas Jefferson	1779–1781	John Buchanan Floyd	1849–1852
Thomas Nelson, Jr.	1781	Joseph Johnson	1852–1856
Benjamin Harrison	1781–1784	Henry Alexander Wise	1856–1860
Patrick Henry	1784–1786	John Letcher	1860–1864
Edmund Randolph	1786–1788	William Smith	1864–1865
Beverley Randolph	1788–1791	Francis H. Pierpont	1865–1868
Henry Lee	1791–1794	Henry H. Wells	1868–1869
Robert Brooke	1794–1796	Gilbert C. Walker	1869–1874
James Wood	1796–1799	James Lawson Kemper	1874–1878
James Monroe	1799–1802	Frederick W. M. Holliday	1878–1882
John Page	1802–1805	William Evelyn Cameron	1882-1886
William H. Cabell	1805–1808	Fitzhugh Lee	1886–1890
John Tyler, Sr.	1808–1811	Philip W. McKinney	1890–1894
James Monroe	1811	Charles T. O'Ferrall	1894–1898
George William Smith	1811	J. Hoge Tyler	1898–1902
Peyton Randolph	1811–1812	Andrew Jackson Montague	1902–1906
James Barbour	1812–1814	Claude A. Swanson	1906–1910
Wilson Cary Nicholas	1814–1816	William Hodges Mann	1910–1914
James Patton Preston	1816–1819	Henry Carter Stuart	1914–1918
Thomas Mann Randolph	1819–1822	Westmoreland Davis	1918–1922
James Pleasants, Jr.	1822–1825	E. Lee Trinkle	1922–1926
John Tyler	1825-1827	Harry Flood Byrd	1926–1930
Willliam B. Giles	1827–1830	John G. Pollard	1930–1934
John Floyd	1830–1834	George C. Perry	1934–1938
Littleton Waller Tazewell	1834–1836	James H. Price	1938–1942
Wyndham Robertson	1836-1837	Colgate W. Darden, Jr.	1942–1946
David Campbell	1837–1840	William M. Tuck	1946–1950
Thomas W. Gilmer	1840–1841	John S. Battle	1950–1954
John M. Patton	1841	Thomas B. Stanley	1954–1958
John Rutherford	1841–1842	J. Lindsay Almond, Jr.	1958–1962
John Mumford Gregory	1842–1843	Albertis S. Harrison	1962–1966
James McDowell	1843–1846	Mills E. Godwin, Jr.	1966–

PEOPLE AND VIRGINIA

Nathaniel Bacon

Sir William Berkeley

James Blair

Harry F. Byrd

William Byrd, II

Dabney Carr

Sir Thomas Dale

Robert Dinwiddie

Benjamin Harrison

William H. Harrison

Patrick Henry

Archer M. Huntington

Thomas Jefferson

Joseph E. Johnston

Francis Lightfoot Lee

Henry Lee

Richard Henry Lee

Robert E. Lee

Cyrus Hall McCormick

James Madison

John Marshall

George Mason

James Monroe

Pocahontas

Chief Powhatan

Sir Walter Raleigh

John Rolfe

John Smith

Alexander Spotswood

James E. B. Stuart

Zachary Taylor

John Tyler

Lord de la Warre

Booker T. Washington

George Washington

Martha Custis Washington

Woodrow Wilson

George Wythe

PRONUNCIATION GUIDE

Appalachian	Ap pa *lay* chun
Appomattox	Ap pa *ma* tux
Chesapeake	*Chess* a peak
Culpeper	*Kul* pe per
Holston	*Hole* stun
Kecoughtan	*Keck* o tan
Kilmarnock	Kill *mar* nuk
Massanutten	Mass a *nuh* tun
Monticello	Mon ti *sell* o
Piedmont	*Peed* mont
Pocahontas	Po cah *hon* tus
Potomac	Pah *toe* muk
Powhatan	Pow a *tan*
Rappahannock	Rap a *ha* nuk
Roanoke	*Roe* a noke
Shenandoah	Shen an *doe* a
Staunton	*Stan* tun
Susquehanna	Sus kwi *ha* na
Tangier	Tan *geer*

INDEX

123

126

The Author

MICHAEL FROME is one of the country's foremost writers on travel and conservation. For the past twenty years, he has lived in Virginia with his family. He knows the state well and loves the beauty and variety of its land — from ocean to mountain. He and his two sons have traveled all over Virginia by car, canoe, horseback and on foot.

Mr. Frome serves on the Governor's Travel Development Committee and the Northern Virginia Conservation Council. He is the author of four adult books and numerous articles for national newspapers and magazines.

STATES OF THE NATION

The "States of the Nation" books provide young readers with an exciting, current profile of each state in the Union.

Within the borders of a state, one finds an individual place that has developed and grown historically, geographically and culturally to become shaped and molded to what it is today. These books explore the character and special qualities of the state, its unique features, and who and what contributed to its making.

To present a vivid, fresh portrayal of each state demanded a thoughtful selection of authors. We have chosen writers who know their state personally, who have a special feeling for it, and who write about it with liveliness, enthusiasm and authority.

Each book in the series has had a careful, step-by-step check with a leading state consultant. An extensive reference section at the back of each book includes basic facts and statistics, a chronological synopsis of history, governors and famous people, a pronunciation guide, and a comprehensive index.

MICHIGAN
by Russel B. Nye

OREGON
by Iris Noble

VIRGINIA
by Michael Frome

VIRGINIA'S COUNTIES

DATE DUE			
			ALESCO